Belle Weather

Also by Celia Rivenbark

Stop Dressing Your Six-Year-Old Like a Skank

We're Just Like You, Only Prettier

Bless Your Heart, Tramp

Belle Weather

Mostly Sunny with a Chance of ❧ Scattered Hissy Fits ❧

Celia Rivenbark

St. Martin's Press

New York

www.stmartins.com

Design by Kathryn Parise

ISBN-13: 978-0-312-36299-7
ISBN-10: 0-312-36299-4

First Edition: August 2008

10 9 8 7 6 5 4 3 2 1

For Nan Graham

Friend, mentor, and the most authentic belle of them all

Contents

Part 1: On the House
1

Part II: Just Kid-ding
79

Part III: It's Raining Men
(Must Be Why My Joints Ache)
159

Part IV: (I'm So Totally) Random Thoughts
211

Part 1

∂ On the House ∂

1

"I Love You, You're Perfect, Now Change!"

For weeks, we'd told the real estate agent that we were just bat-shit crazy about contemporary homes. Hubby and I drooled over the cheap, sleek Scandinavian crap in the Ikea catalogue. I imagined wearing all-black or all-white outfits and hosting pristine dinner parties where everyone had a white plate with a single perfect olive on it and nothing else. Our guests would laugh in a throaty, cultured, contemporary way as they pondered the origin of this perfect olive.

Modern! Get it, Ms. Real Estate Agent with the Lexus SUV? No Colonials, no Tudors, not so much as a '50s ranch house for us. We wanted the kind of cool-cat, minimalist style you don't see much in small Southern towns unless it belongs to the snooty art professor at the local college and his life partner. We weren't a gay couple, obviously, but we sure were house-shopping like one.

So my forty-something agent slipped on her Ferragamos, fussed with her helmet hair in the mirror, tugged on her imitation St. John knit suit and set her mind to finding us, the Southern freaks, the modern house of our dreams.

She did a tremendous job, except for the time she apparently drank too much Robitussin and drove us to a split-level Brady Bunch house that made us gag and whine.

"This ain't contemporary at all," I chided her.

Hiccup.

One day, deep into the fourth month of house hunting, she drove us to a new development of contemporary homes and we oohed and aahed over the white walls and steely solemnity. The living room in the model home was straight off the cover of the Crate & Barrel catalogue. You know the one: white couch, black fuzzy pillows, and that single, perfect hot-pink zinnia providing the only color in the room. It's so tasteful it makes you want to throw up.

"Well?" real estate lady said, sweeping her arms grandly. "What do you think? Is this the one? It is, isn't it? I just know it. It's the one."

"Well, sorta," hubby said.

"Not so much," I said.

Real estate lady tried mightily not to show the disappointment she was feeling. She'd given us her best shot for four months and it wasn't good enough.

The next week, hubby and I got lost on a one-way street in an old section of town. And there, on this street that no one knew about, was the perfect house with a sign in the yard.

We called real estate lady and asked her to find out all she could about it.

She was so excited that she drove over immediately to the perfect house. But when she pulled up, her face was ashen.

"You OK?" I asked.

"But (sob) this (sob) isn't even close to (sob) contemporary!"

"Oh, yeah, about that . . . ," I said.

We stood on the sidewalk in front of the perfect house and realized that it was nothing like we had described. Instead, it was a two-story Federal-style house that was ninety years old and needed a ton of work.

"Isn't it beautiful?" I asked.

"Uh-huh," real estate lady managed. "But it's old, really old, and it looks as if it might need, uh, some work."

"Don't worry!" hubby crowed. "I can do a lot of the work myself." Well, not really. Hubby isn't what you'd call handy. The one time I asked him to hang a picture in our apartment, it took twelve hours and a six-pack and even then that picture was crookedy 'til the day we moved out.

But we had House Fever and all that we could think about

was moving in. There would be an offer, a counteroffer, and tons of inspections.

Looking back on it, I'm fairly certain the inspector was on crack when he proclaimed our house had "good bones." Perhaps he simply meant that he'd run into some while underneath the house, perhaps the brittle, calcified remnants of whatever handyman had been sucked into the murk for whatever repair long before we were born.

With the purchase of this old house, gone was the notion of the olive dinner party. This was more redneck Riviera, a home for oyster roasts and third cousins passing out and sleeping in the yard. It was purely, deeply Southern and we loved it. You could practically hear Olympia Dukakis imploring Sally Field to smack Shirley Maclaine across the face in the big backyard. It was *Steel Magnolias* and *Ya-Ya*s rolled into one and, looking at the two enormous pecan trees in the yard, I couldn't believe I'd ever thought we could go modern.

Nope, this was our house and we would love it and care for it and raise our baby in it and not even care when the basement filled with six feet of water during hurricanes. Which it did.

Friends who visited our new old house always said the same thing: "Did you ever see that movie? Gosh, what was it called? Had Shelley Long in it, maybe Michael Keaton? Or was it Tom Hanks?"

"Are you talking about *The Money Pit*?" we'd ask.

And, of course, they were.

"That's the one! This house reminds me of that house in the movie. Hahahaha!"

Yes, hahahahahahaha, indeed.

We moved in and began the long process of renovation, at one point deciding that it would be a whole lot easier to just check into the hospital and have repeated elective surgeries until it was safe to come home again.

First up, the kitchen.

When you set out to gut a ninety-year-old kitchen, you have to be prepared for the occasional unforeseen challenge, or, as we like to call it, "rot."

"See," the contractor-guy explained, as though talking to two small, dimwitted children, "water is the enemy of wood."

I was afraid he was going to say, "Now say it after me" just like my eighth-grade science teacher did.

Water, it turns out, hates wood like Trump hates Rosie. The two spend entire decades fighting inside your walls, until one day a big, noisy tool exposes them just like a deputy holding a flashlight and shining it into the backseat when you're parked at the junior high ball field. Oh, sorry. Where was I?

We had a crackerjack team working on our old house. There was Darrell and Damon and Donnie Ray and Dion, the head guy.

It's a "D" thing; try to understand.

Each morning, the boys would roll up in assorted trucks, fumble for a cigarette or ten and walk up and down looking at the rear of the house.

They'd always shake their heads, calling to mind the country expression I grew up with that applied to times when Aunt Elna Jay or whomever had "the cancer."

In the rural South, "the cancer" surgery is always followed by a report from some kin proclaiming that "They opened Elna Jay up but when they took a look at her insides, well, they just sewed her right back up." It's dramatic, always accompanied by a stitching-in-the-air motion and it never fails to elicit a chorus of "I swanee"s or even a hushed "Sweet Jesus" or two.

This is how the D team looked at the kitchen addition and renovation. Even the prospect of a complete demo of the ninety-year-old kitchen wasn't enough to cheer them up. It was a gargantuan task ahead of them, not made any easier by the first day's revelation that a very large dead rat would have to be dealt with when they pried up some boards.

Darrell promptly threw up his barbecue sandwich and Sun Drop and I realized that this was a sensitive bunch.

I came to know the crew, and the many sub-crews, very well. And, they, in turn got to know me well. I adored these men and wished that I could've fed them biscuits and gravy every day but, since I no longer had any semblance of a kitchen, that was pretty much impossible.

After three months of male bonding, I'd gotten used to the house crawling with men whose names began with D.

Everything was going great, that is, until one very unfortunate morning.

I thought they'd all gone in their many trucks to the lumberyard to fetch wood to replace the challenged section of the day.

Alone at last, and happily wandering in robe and slippers

from room to room in my suddenly silent house, I, well, let slip an ill wind, so to speak. It is not an exaggeration to say that it was so loud and resonant as to threaten the very newly poured foundation of my kitchen. Rebar-schmebar; something's gonna blow!

And then, it happened. On the other side of a thin piece of plywood that had been nailed up to protect the rest of the house from lung-clogging mountains of dust, I heard an embarrassed shuffling of feet and fake coughing.

Precious Lord, take me now.

And, no, it matters not a whit that kings and queens do it. How could I have been so reckless? They always leave at least one man behind in case a new episode of rot breaks out.

I realize that this confession may startle those of you who assume that a Southern flower such as myself would be incapable of committing such a vile act but I can only be perfectly truthful with y'all and say that there is a first time for everything.

I've known many men over the years who claim never to have heard their wives expel anything noisy from their bodies other than perhaps an excited and grateful squeal during lovemaking but these men have *no idea* what happens when they finally clear out and these women can, at last, behave as nature intended.

People, we are human!

As I stood, frozen in horror and shame, I was filled with regret for the previous night's dinner. For just as water and wood are a really bad combination, so are a fish sandwich and Cheddar Pepper Poppers from Sonic.

I couldn't be sure, but I thought the D Team was looking at me differently over the next few weeks. A few of them began to loudly burp as though to make me feel more comfortable in my own home.

Their motives were pure and primal, I suppose. It's like, in the wild, when one animal does something to indicate to the other that they can be friends. It would have been inappropriate for us to sniff one another's naughties so this was the best they could do to let me know that they understood we were all human beings full of hopes and dreams and flatulence.

Because I'm not one to suffer in silence, I unburdened myself to my girlfriends, who were completely sympathetic, as it turns out. In fact, the more I told the story, the better I felt.

One friend confided that for months, during construction of an addition to an upstairs bedroom, she had to rearrange her entire day around her poops.

"God almighty, I had to drink coffee by five a.m. just so I could take a private dump by six and they wouldn't know about it."

One older gentleman who had read my confession in a newspaper column (I told y'all I have *no* secrets) ventured out of his parlor and away from his Victrola long enough to inform me that he had been married three times and none of his wives had ever "committed such a despicable act."

Hey, it didn't exactly take the team from "CSI: Texarkana" to figure out the cause o' death of those old broads: They blew up! After all, y'all, gas has to go somewhere. If you live with a, pardon me, old fart who is monitoring your every gas bubble, it's not going to be long before you explode.

I'm just saying.

2

Stone Love

Granite's Not Just for Tombstones Anymore

⌘

Deep into the renovation of our kitchen and the addition of a laundry room and patio, we realized that the world is essentially divided into two types of people: (A) Those who have undertaken a costly and not altogether necessary renovation or remodeling job that involves the moving, elimination, or relocation of perfectly good walls and (B) those who are sane.

Insanity had become the order of the day as weeks stretched into months on the remodeling of This Old Mother-Humpin' House.

I was starting to lose friends because—and this is the dirty little secret of renovation—when you live in a home that's undergoing major work, you can no longer relate to people who aren't going through the same thing.

If you don't believe me, consider this conversation between me and my *former* best friend Dawn Marie, which I will now report as close to verbatim as possible.

Dawn Marie: "Celia, I am just beside myself with worry. I think I'm going to have to leave my husband. Last night, Chuck told me that he has been having an affair for nearly eight months with little Chuckie's preschool teacher!"

Me: "Wow. That's a tough decision, er, Dawn. It's kind of like what I've been going through this week. Do I really need the Wolf range with the six-burner cooktop or should I just admit that four is enough, use the extra dough for the pewter-colored pot filler, and get on with my life?"

Dawn Marie: "You're not even listening to me. This is the worst thing that has ever happened to me in my whole life and all you can think about is your stupid new kitchen and your stupid wood laminate floor!"

Me: "Whoa, bee-atch! You are *so* unfair; you know we've been lying awake at night wondering about tile or hardwood, hardwood or tile, which way to go? Laminate? *Laminate?* What do I look like, the little frikkin' match girl? So now who's the one not listening?"

So I hated to admit it but it was true: Dawn Marie was pretty much a jerk. I believe we can all agree on that.

Agreeing on granite for the countertops, now that was a real problem.

Who knew that a big, dumb rock could cost so much? But as the guts of the kitchen began to take shape, I learned from People Who Know Stuff that all granite is not created equal.

While I leaned toward saving money by buying a slab from the scruffy guy wearing the wife-beater and selling cheap granite from the back of a flatbed truck beside the railroad tracks (and who promised to toss in two free tombstones with purchase, I kid you not), I began to suspect that scruffy guy's claim that "It fell off'n the back of a truck" was probably not altogether true.

As we say in the South, I didn't know anything about this granite's people. It was triflin' stolen-ass granite and would probably not even pass the lemon test. (Hell-o, it's where you squeeze a few drops on the granite to see if it turns dark, thus exposing you as having loser-quality granite.)

Granite had completely taken over my life. I dreamed about it, talked about it, and eventually even "visited it" as my kitchen consultant insisted.

"You have to visit your granite," she said, speaking slowly as if she was talking to the type of person who would stupidly buy Italian granite off the Internet only to discover it was from Italy, Kentucky.

Granite comes from many fine sources throughout the world, the kitchen lady explained. It's like a billion years old, formed when the earth's crust cooled, way before dinosaurs and Andy Rooney roamed the earth.

The kitchen lady said granite is carved out of a mountain and polished with diamonds. What can I say? This made me giddy. The word "diamonds," much like the phrase "all you can eat" always makes my heart skip a beat.

I finally selected a sample of something called "verde peacock" which is Spanish, I believe, for "green peacock."

"Ooooooh," the kitchen lady cooed, stroking her hand over my granite sample. "You have excellent taste. Most people just choose the uba tuba and it makes me want to cry."

At that precise moment, I saw the price difference and I was the one who wanted to cry. Uba tuba was way less expensive than verde peacock because it's the most common granite. Uba tuba went to public school and felt damned lucky to graduate with at least the ability to drive a car and perhaps weld something. Verde peacock was more refined, snooty liberal arts college material, and it was going to be mine if I had to sell one of my husband's organs to buy it.

Hey, it's not like he needs two kidneys, am I right?

Kitchen lady excitedly told me that she'd make the arrangements for us to visit the granite.

"Fabulous!" I said, envisioning a trip to its exotic land of origin. I'd done enough research to know the best granite comes from Italy, Spain, France, and Greece.

"Honey," I said to my husband, who had actually fallen asleep standing up in front of a display of travertine tiles, "Wake up! We're going to visit our granite. It's very exotic so we'll probably have to travel a long ways."

"Ka-ching," he muttered sleepily.

"Oh, no, don't worry," the kitchen lady said, patting him on the small of his back, right where I imagined the surgical scar would probably be some day. "Actually the granite you selected is a tad closer to home."

"Really? Where?" I asked.

"Well, actually, your granite is in Myrtle Beach."

Good-bye Louvre, hello Dixie Stampede. I was irrationally disappointed.

"You'll need to schedule an appointment to visit it," the kitchen lady continued.

"Say who?" my husband said. This is the Southern man's response to anything that causes momentary confusion or puzzlement.

I sighed, rolled my eyes, and jumped in to fix this.

"I apologize for my husband. I believe what he meant to say was, 'Do what?'"

Well. Some people just aren't fluent in Southern. I'm used to being a translator. It's a gift.

Because we live just a little over an hour's drive from Myrtle Beach, this was going to be easy. Still, it was hard for me to reconcile the Myrtle Beach I knew, which was heavy on factory outlets, fish camps, and "gentlemen's clubs" with the rich, elegant verde peacock I had fallen for.

I began to think of our granite as a kitten at the animal shelter, waiting for its rightful owners to come save it from a grim fate. I would take this granite home and it would be safe from ever having to see another human being wearing a shirt with "My Other Ride Is Your Mom" on the front.

It would be grateful and perform admirably over the years. The kitchen lady was excited about scheduling the visit because, as she explained, it was a bit like an adoption process.

We visited the granite and I wept because it was so pretty. Really. I stood there in a gravel parking lot while a guy driving a forklift kept my slab suspended in the air and I walked around it about eighteen times. I had the distinct impression that if I walked around one more time, he was going to drop it on my foot.

But this was our time together, me and my granite, and it was love at first sight. The tears came out of nowhere, unless you count the peri-menopausal haze that I reside in for most of the day.

As my eyes welled, my nine-year-old said I was embarrassing her and I told her that Mommy needed a moment *and* Mommy had forgotten to take her mood-altering drugs that morning so what the hell was her problem, anyway?

On the way out, I saw a woman caressing her (snicker) uba tuba slab and talking to it.

"Hey, at least I'm not talking to granite like that poor soul," I told Sophie, whose look told me that she wished she could trade me in for a sane mommy.

"Mom," she said, with an irritated tone that I instantly recognized from my own tween years, "If we stay much longer, I'm going to start my period. Let's go!"

Oh, snap! I have always admired sarcasm in the very young.

The granite installation was subbed out to men whose

names did not all begin with "D." And since they were able to do the entire installation in less than a day, I didn't even get a chance to fart on them.

Their loss, right?

3

Possum Chokes on Packing Peanuts

Gross Film at Eleven

In the South, we're used to varmints, but we sugarcoat everything, so we never use the word "cockroach" to refer to that icky, skittering blur of a bug that runs when you turn the kitchen light on.

We call these "water bugs," which sounds somehow more genteel. Occasionally, we call them "palmetto bugs," which sounds downright charming, as if they march about with palm fronds for hair and carry tiny little glasses of sweet tea on a tray.

Whatever they are, we all have them and it has nothing to

do with how clean your house is. I've seen two-inch water bugs skittering around the pool of an oceanfront mansion and I've seen their rowdy cousins hanging out in the sidewalk cracks outside the seediest riverfront bar.

Not long ago, we were at a fancy party given at the home of our one set of rich friends. The house was gorgeous, like something out of *Southern Living*, which defines high style to any right-thinking Southerner. The buffet table was resplendent with Chantilly sterling, naturally, and as I reached for a cheese puff, I saw little legs skittering across the Battenburg lace tablecloth and heading straight for the carving station.

I discreetly informed our hostess that there was a water bug hiding near the au jus in her grandmama's heirloom gravy boat and she might want to get that taken care of. Make no mistake; this is the spinach-on-your-front-tooth in the South. We want to know when there has been a sighting so we can fix it.

No screams, no squeals, no apologies. The hostess simply plastered a beatific smile on her face, covered the bug with a monogrammed napkin and, in the single most graceful pest removal moment I have witnessed, picked up gravy boat and covered bug, announcing that she needed to replenish the au jus. Nobody knew a thing.

Southern women are remarkably good at dealing with bugs as long as no one calls them cockroachs. That is simply unsavory.

I'm personally good at dealing with wasps. One spring day,

I opened the windows of my little home office and discovered that while I'd been passing an uneventful winter, killer wasps had been merrily constructing a community so large it deserved its own sidewalks and city sewer.

The wasps flooded my office and lapped my head like it was the infield at Daytona. I looked for something to spray at them but all that was handy was a can of Lemon Pledge.

So I sprayed 'em good, but it didn't help. The wasps continued to buzz, dip, and torture me, plus now they had much shinier wings.

Finally, I ran downstairs and found a rusty can of Hot Shot, which I sprayed wildly about the room with the door only open enough to put my arm through.

One by one, they began to sputter and flop, collapsing against the baseboards.

Of course, it would've been a really good idea to close the windows at some point but I wasn't thinking clearly. I'd just inhaled most of the contents of a nine-ounce can of Pledge and a can of Hot Shot so old that it bragged about "reducing the threat of polio." New wasp recruits buzzed around, while, horrifyingly, the "dead" wasps began to come alive again, humming and wriggling. Fortunately, they were hung over, so I was able to clobber them with hubby's size thirteen basketball shoes, wearing one on each hand like the mittens o' death. A final wasp struggled to fly in my peripheral vision and I invited it to, yes, go ahead, make my day.

Sadly, we don't handle larger pests with nearly as much skill.

When our cat brought a mouse into our upstairs bathroom

late one night, hubby and I both screamed and slammed the door.

"We can't just leave them in there," I moaned to Hubby. "At least turn the light off."

"Nonsense," he said, "The bulb will burn out on its own eventually."

This has been our approach to rodent control for years, but there finally came a time when we knew it was time to call a professional.

A possum, his sides bursting with Styrofoam peanuts he must've foolishly eaten while we were unpacking new faucets for the kitchen, had up and died under our house in mid-renovation.

Possums are powerfully stupid, it turns out.

In the midst of all the work, the possum had gotten confused and mistaken the packing peanuts for something that could actually be digested.

Because of his location, in a crawlspace under our house, we had no intention of going after him. He would have to be removed by someone who wouldn't shudder and squeal and go "Ewwww." The D boys were out; ever since the rat incident I'd realized they didn't do varmints.

So I looked in the Yellow Pages and, a few phone calls later, I finally found someone who specialized in varmint removal, although he was loathe to use "the V word" as he prissily called it.

"Vince" was extremely professional and official-sounding

when I talked to him on the phone. Bottom line, he said, it would cost about $250 to remove the possum from under our house.

"Two hundred and fifty dollars!" I screeched. "Are you planning to hire Celine Dion to sing at his frikkin' funeral? Just go up under the house, drag his dead ass out, and take him away."

Vince then launched into a discussion of "humane" methods of removal.

"Look," I said as calmly as I could because, let's face it, I needed Vince more than he needed me at this point. "The possum is dead. *Dead!* I don't care if you go all Abu Ghraib, put a leash around his neck and smoke a cigarette with your leg propped up on his haunches. Just get him the hell outta here!"

Once Vince actually listened and realized the possum had waddled on over to that great other-side-of-the-road in the sky, I was sure the fee would drop dramatically, but I was wrong.

"On the initial investigation, we will ascertain as to the particular species of the possum . . ."

Sweet Lord above. Deliver me from a worldly pest control expert. Whatever happened to the good old days when I could just dangle a twelve-pack in front of a passing redneck and not only get the varmint removed but also get a damn good start on a deck on the back of the house?

I tried again.

"I don't care what species he is, on account of why? Hmmm. Oh, yes! That's right. HE'S DEAD!"

"Ma'am," said Vince, "Just because he's dead doesn't mean that he's not deserving of respectful treatment."

"Vince," I said, "are you high?"

I realized that the possum would just have to stay where he was. I'd run into Vince's type once before when I was shopping for an exterminator.

We'd had a little problem with those water bugs I just mentioned. Summer in the South is peak season and if they got any larger, my kid was going to put bonnets and gloves on them and invite them to her little tea parties.

"We don't call ourselves exterminators anymore," huffed "Clark," the man in the eco-green Polo shirt. He sounded genuinely hurt.

"It's like calling a funeral director an undertaker," he said. "It's called pest control now."

"Hey, just 'cause the cat had kittens in the oven doesn't mean they're biscuits," I said, repeating the wisdom of my Great Aunt Sudavee or Suzanne Sugarbaker, I forget which.

"What does that mean?" asked Clark.

"It means I don't care what you call it, just get these water bugs dead. And I don't want you to just kill them. I want them to *suffer* a little first. Can you do that?"

Clark-the-pompous-pest-guy looked at me as if I was nuts.

"OK, OK," I said. "You drive a hard bargain. I'll toss in an extra twelve-pack if you can promise a little suffering."

"I don't drink," he said rather stiffly.

Of course he didn't. Unless it was, perhaps, an unassuming pinot noir accompanied by some fried frou-frou and a side of "I'm better than you."

It was a varmint, of sorts, that recently reminded me that despite all the talk of blended populations and such, we Southerners are still different from the rest of the world. And not just because the people who work at Chick-fil-A always tell you to "Have a blessed day."

Maybe it's because we live in perpetual fear of monster hurricanes and unsweet tea, both plenty scary in their own way.

The Defining Varmint Moment happened when I was visiting a new friend who had moved from Long Island, which, as I have experienced firsthand, has an entirely different take on iced tea.

I was saying good-bye to my new Yankee friend on her front porch when I spied a snake, about four feet long, slithering its way toward my car.

Southern women do not like snakes. No, no. What I meant to say is: SOUTHERN WOMEN DO NOT LIKE SNAKES!!!!

So I screamed. And so did Phyllis, although frankly she came in a little late, now that I think about it.

"Snake!" I shrieked.

"Snake!" Phyllis shrieked.

"Get a hoe!" I shrieked

"Huh?" Phyllis said.

Fortunately, at this moment, Phyllis' husband and their neighbor, also a recent Yankee transplant, walked into the yard.

Relief flooded over me like butter on a hot biscuit. Everything was going to be OK.

The Yankee neighbor's garage door was up and I could see a fine array of Snake Killing Implements hanging neatly on pegboard.

"Get a hoe!" I shouted to the men, who, I'd noticed, weren't really moving as fast as I thought they should. "Snake!!"

The men looked perplexed.

"A hoe?" said the neighbor who was wearing a jumpsuit that I suddenly found annoying as hell.

Why were these two men looking at me as if I'd asked them to help me strangle a basket of kittens?

"Oh, he's not a threat," said icky jumpsuited neighbor guy. "Snakes actually protect us from other harmful pests."

I could've sworn I saw the snake pause to laugh at this, while on his way to curl around my front tire in a completely gross and spineless snaky way.

"*Get a hoe!*" I repeated, thinking that at least Phyllis' husband would take this seriously.

But he'd also become Johnny Environmentalist and was babbling about rodent control and other Utter Crap. At this point, the snake appeared to be outright guffawing.

And then it hit me: I needed a Bubba. My whole life, Southern men have come to my rescue, but this wasn't something that translated geographically. Where I'm from, if a woman hollers "Snake!" at least four Bubbas will magically appear, hoes in hand, and you're looking at snake puddin' in under ten seconds.

The snake, hearing all of this, slithered away to romp some more in his happy, Bubba-free neighborhood.

"Fuhgeddaboutit," I heard him hiss.

4

Shocked Smart? Nope, But I'm Plenty Grounded

At some point during the renovation of an old house, someone is going to strongly suggest that your electrical system needs to be updated. They will use grave tones and speak of "code violations," and "serious chance of electrical fire" and "how I really need a Hawaiian vacation with my second family."

"You're just saying that scary stuff because you want me to pay you many thousands of dollars," I told one electrician who had arrived to bid on the job.

"No, ma'am," he said, "I'm just saying that scary stuff be-cause every time I flip on a light switch in your house, I get a shock that erases my memory of the past fifteen years. Who the hell am I, anyway?"

"Oh, man up!" I told the wussy electrician. "They don't make electrical systems like this puppy anymore."

"It's called knob-and-tube," he said, "and they haven't really made it since, hmmmmm, nineteen–and–twenty-two. Then again, how would I know that? *Who am I?*"

Another electrician arrived to give an estimate and was equally horrified by the state of our system.

"None of your outlets are even grounded," he whined.

"Good. We're not grounded either," I said. "If we were, we wouldn't be spending our kid's entire college education fund on Beanie Babies from eBay. Oh, sure, they may be out of style now, but they're coming back one day and we're gonna be sittin' pretty. Here. Take this unicorn. Could be worth a lot of money one day."

The third electrician to put in a bid couldn't speak English. This isn't a deal-breaker for me because I have an uncanny ability to communicate with people no matter what their lan-guage. In this case, it was Spanish.

"Que mucho?" I asked brightly after the electrician had made his final trip over, around, and under the house.

He pointed toward our dark and spooky basement, shud-dered, and then screamed out, "El Diablo!!!"

I've seen enough bad Westerns to know that this is Spanish for "The hair dryer!"

"Que?" I asked. There wasn't a hair dryer down there. What a goof this guy was.

He ran from the house and leapt into his truck and I happily added his large battery-operated lantern and clipboard to a box I was filling with all the things that people who give estimates leave behind. Tape measures, a few levels, a voltage meter . . . One guy had even left a very nice sky blue fleece jacket. Was our house so awful that people didn't even want to come back and claim their belongings?

I believe the answer was "Sí."

We finally settled on electrician candidate No. 4, whose name was Mike. He was a man of few words, but when he spoke, his words really mattered, kind of like that chick who narrates *Desperate Housewives* and always makes me want to say, "If you're so damned smart, why are you dead?"

But Mike, the man of few words, said the magic ones as far as I was concerned:

"Just knock $500 off whatever your lowest guy says and I'll do the job for that."

Suh-weet!

As it turned out, Mike was a fabulous electrician who had a very dependable stable of helper-bees, including one who looked, spoke, and sounded exactly like Gomer Pyle, U.S.M.C., right on down to a heartfelt "Shazam!" when he saw the now-famous knob-and-tube setup in the attic.

Unfortunately, as with many in-demand professionals, Mike and company were also working on roughly forty-eight other electrical jobs at the same time, so there would be days when he didn't show up at all. This is an unfortunate reality in the contracting world.

Even my beloved "D'boyz" had left me for a couple of weeks to finish another woman's patio, a fact that left me weirdly depressed.

"Look," Dion finally said, after I'd called him twenty-seven times on his cell phone begging him to come over, "Don't you realize that when we're here, she's probably feeling as if we've abandoned *her*?"

"But I don't care about *her*," I sniffled. "I just want you guys here!"

They returned the next day.

Dion gave me a patient smile, patted me on the shoulder, and said, "Sometimes it's hard letting go, even for a little while." I pulled myself together and we shared a cigarette.

"I guess you're right," I sniffled. "It doesn't mean that you've forgotten us. Look, I'm sorry. It's not you; it's me."

As Mike and his helpers set about the task of rewiring the entire house, installing some newfangled gadgets called "breakers" and such, I began to realize that the end was in sight.

Finally, on a warm Spring morning, Mike announced that, after six weeks representing roughly twenty hours of work, we were "good to go."

I was ecstatic! The "breaker box" was labeled all neat and shiny and there were grounded outlets and something called GFCIs everywhere.

"That prevents electrical shock when you're in kitchens and bathrooms," Mike said proudly. He had made our house o' horrors safe for inhabitants for the first time since the Hoover administration.

And things were pretty, too. Mike and Gomer had installed more than forty different lights in the new kitchen alone: a chandelier, assorted spots, cans, under-cabinet, halogens, pendants, most with dimmer switches so you could change the entire mood of the room from bright (Velveeta shells and cheese with kids) to romantic (Velveeta shells and cheese with kids and hubby).

After Mike left, I walked from room to room, upstairs and down, feeling safe from any electrical threat and admiring the shiny new smoke detectors Mike had installed in every room. No, nothing could hurt me now.

Nothing, except my dryer, that is.

See, Mike had installed a new 220 line for our dryer because it pulls a lot more electricity than most things in the house. A whole lot more. To put this in layman's terms: Think of normal house current as Mary-Kate Olsen. Now think of the power needed for a dryer as Pamela Anderson. There. I think you have it.

With the new laundry room done, there was just one thing that needed to happen. Mike had entrusted me to pick up a new dryer cord because the old one wasn't "code."

Naturally.

I couldn't believe that I had my washer/dryer back. For exactly five months, I had been hauling fifty pounds of laundry across town to the Laundromat.

The good news was, these weekly trips had helped my

Spanish immensely. Face it; three years of high school Spanish had only equipped me to say, "My uncle can ride the unicycle!" while five months at the Laundromat had made me truly fluent. My new Hispanic friends even taught me how to use the water-extracting gizmo. It's called the "Bock" and there's a cartoon panel of illustrations showing an obviously brain-dead woman jumping up and down because the Bock has changed her life.

I had noticed that my new Laundromat friends tended to laugh and point at me often while saying things that I have interpreted to be either, "The blond American woman! She has such shiny quarters" or, possibly, "She is OK, but I wish she'd shut up about her uncle who rides the unicycle."

I'd miss my "amigas" but it was time to say good-bye to weekly barbecue sandwiches from the restaurant next door and back-to-back *Matlock* episodes on the Laundromat TV.

The washer/dryer were in place and all that was stopping me was this dryer cord thing. Piece. Of. Cake.

What happened next is a blur. I remember trying to get the dryer cord out of its packaging and, when I couldn't get it out, I just decided to plug it into the new outlet while it was still all wrapped up to see if it was the right size. Unfortunately, there's some sort of grounding wire that has to be in the right place.

Long story short, blue flames shot across the room, my hair stood on end, and my fingers turned black (and not that cool new shade by OPI).

My husband, hearing my screams from the next room, said,

"What's for dinner?" No, no. What he said was, "Why do you look like that? And what's for dinner?"

The dryer plug fused itself together and that goo fused to the wall outlet and Mike confirmed the next morning that I was lucky to be alive so I could finish paying him.

This was all quite scary and foolish, but I kept thinking, what if I'd turn out like John Travolta in *Phenomenon* (consult local listings; trust me, it's on somewhere). In the movie, Travolta's character sees a bright blue electrical light just like I saw coming at me from a dryer outlet and, well, he turns brilliant.

A former doofus, much like me, Travolta is shocked-smart!

He learns Portuguese in twenty minutes and can explain all sorts of theories that would kick Einstein's shaggy ass.

So, I sat in the laundry room while my hair silently smoked, and waited for the genius to come.

When it still hadn't come a few hours later, I called my friend, Christy Kramer, to complain. CK has watched every movie ever made with John Travolta in it, even the sucky ones. Right away, she reminded me that Travolta dies at the end of the movie from sheer intellectual overload.

"Dude, he dies," CK said. "Be careful what you ask for."

She was right. So maybe it's better to stay mediocre. So far, there is absolutely no evidence that my near-death dryer experience has done anything to make me smarter. In fact, it may have had the opposite effect because, the other day, I actually heard myself laugh out loud at an episode of *That's So Raven*.

Now that's frikkin' scary.

5

Mulch Ado About Nothing

Although things were taking shape inside the house, it was becoming obvious that the massive renovation had taken its toll on our yard. A big-ass Dumpster had sat outside the kitchen window for months. Every few weeks, it would fill up and we'd have to pay many hundreds of dollars to get it hauled off and replaced with another.

At first, having my own Dumpster was just about the coolest thing that had happened in my life.

Every redneck dreams of having her own Dumpster to "chuck" things into. Never again would I be forced to drive the hickory-scented remains of a barbecued hog carcass all over town while trying to find a store without a night security guard on Dumpster duty. Which I'm here to tell you is nigh unto impossible. Which just makes me think that, on any given Sadday night, there are hordes of redneck men and women cruising the alleys helplessly looking for somewhere to dump the post-party picked-pig carcass. (Incidentally, did you know that it is actually possible to fit a full-grown deer, hooves and all, into the trunk of a Ford Taurus? Don't ask me how I know, I just know. If Ford had jumped on that little tidbit, they'd still be rolling those babies off the assembly line, if you ask me.)

Face it; there are just times when having your own Dumpster is remarkably attractive.

At first, I was magnanimous to our neighbors, offering them to dump whatever accumulated household shit they wanted to into *my* Dumpster, which I had named "Brad" for no particular reason.

The neighbors thought this was great until, one day, the D guys asked me to come outside. Brad was stuffed with an awesome assortment of redneck carnage, including a stained mattress and box spring, assorted neon beer signs that had seen better days, and a taxidermied bear.

"You do realize that you're paying by the load, right?" asked Dion.

"Well," I said, suddenly realizing that my generosity was costing me hundreds of dollars, "Of course I knew that. Do you think I'm stupid?"

"So that's your bear?" Damon asked.

"Hell, yeah, it's my bear," I said. "I'm only throwing him

out because he *so* doesn't go with the stuff I got coming from Pottery Barn."

After a while, the word was out: Brad was no longer available to anyone who didn't live or work in our house. It was just costing too much.

I was sad to see Brad leave but sadder still when I saw what all those months had done to the ground beneath him. My yard looked like *The Killing Fields*. For the first time in my life, I would have to call upon the services of a professional landscaper.

It was a good week for it because the D boys had taken some time off. I learned this after calling Dion late Monday morning and discovering that he was answering his cell phone from the top of the Tower of Terror ride at Walt Disney World.

"You're in Disney World!" I said. "I didn't know you were going to Disney World. When are you coming back? What about my kitchen?"

Dion assured me that he had told me that he was taking the wife and kids to Disney World. He probably had, but I assumed that was going to be after the kitchen was finished.

"Dude," he said, and I could hear him lighting a cigarette, which I'm fairly certain is strictly forbidden on the Tower of Terror, "I'll be back before you know it. Whoa. Gotta go. This thing is wicked scary. Arrrrrgggggghhhhh!!"

The landscaper, whose name was Bo, listened sympathetically to my end of the conversation.

"We can fix all this," Bo said. "I'm gonna work you in between a couple of Chili's and an Applebee's I'm doing."

Sweet. I had a real landscaper guy, the kind that was hired by ginormous mediocre restaurant chains. Maybe he could carve me out a little red chili pepper out of cedar mulch like they do at the restaurant.

While Bo and his all-Hispanic crew, none of whom wanted to hear about my uncle's unicycling prowess, installed truckloads of sod to fill the furrows left by Brad, I realized that it was up to me to do the "pretty part," the flowers and hanging baskets and stuff like that.

At my favorite local plant store, I could have sworn that I heard the bargain-priced asparagus fern that was so handsome whisper, "Pick the begonia, no really, it's much prettier than I."

"Nonsense," I said to the plant, causing a woman to pull her little girl close to her and scoot away.

I plopped the asparagus fern into my cart. When I added a couple of black-eyed Susans, I could've sworn I heard screams.

The clerk had been so hopeful, not knowing about my plant-killing reputation.

"These will come back every year, you know," she said as she rang up the Susans.

"Ha! Not if they know what's good for 'em," I said.

My friends know that I kill plants and have even accused me of watering them with bleach.

"How else could they die so suddenly?" moaned my friend Gray. "It's just not even possible. Maybe you have that Munchausen Syndrome for plants. You kill them for the attention it brings *you*!"

"That's ridiculous. And you need to stop watching so many episodes of *House*."

"No, it's true," she said. "I've never seen anyone who could kill a plant as quickly as you." As Gray spoke, she caressed the brown, wrinkly remnants of my portulaca. Yes, that would be the one that's a member of the cactus family, the one that the nice lady at the plant store swore could tolerate insane Jeffrey Dahmer amounts of abuse.

"We'll just see about that," I thought to myself, wondering, if it was related to the cactus why it would ever need any water at all. I mean it's not as if I have time to become some sort of Henrietta Horticulture. I have a life to live, back issues of *In Touch* to read, important stuff like that.

Here's the great thing about getting older: When you do and say crazy things, nobody gives much of a shit; it's expected.

I've reached the age where I can say and do things that, if I were younger, would land me in the nearest nuthouse doing crayon therapy and weaving dream catchers all day.

Because of this, I told Gray over lunch one day, I had made a life-changing and money-saving decision.

"I'm going to plant plastic flowers in my yard."

Her fork clattered to the floor.

"You can't be serious," she said. "That's what crazy old ladies do."

"I know!" I said, giggling and fumbling for the huge wad of Kleenex that had mysteriously found its way into my purse alongside a "guide to tipping" the size of a playing card. "Isn't it wonderful? Is it dark in here to you? I don't know why restaurants are so dark these days. It's like eating in a damn cave."

Gray was persistent.

"Only tacky people who live in trailer parks plant plastic flowers in their yards," she said.

"Hold on there, Snobby McSnobbypants. I happen to be the only member of my family who has never lived on a chassis so you're hitting a little close to home."

"Sorry, but you can't plant plastic flowers in your yard. It's what poor Yankees do."

Whoa. That was low.

"OK," I said, suddenly having second thoughts. I had noticed how the Yankees who move South, the ones who can't afford to live in those ritzy gated Yankee containment compounds with the golf courses and racquet clubs, will plant plastic flowers.

"How about in containers?" I said. "I've got dozens of empty containers and window boxes left over from all those weenie plants I've coddled over the years."

"Coddled?" Gray shrieked. "Coddled? You barely water them and you've never once fertilized them."

"Well, duh. The boy has to do that."

She thinks she knows so much.

Fortunately, it was about this time that I met Todd, a cute guy who insisted on calling me "ma'am" even though I told him that it made me feel like Miss Daisy. Todd had the perfect solution to my landscaping woes: He'd cover up all that shit with fake cobblestones.

It turns out that this is a fabulous way to deal with an ugly yard. There's a whole world of "hardscaping" out there that I knew nothing about.

Todd could even put a huge eagle design in the patio, if I wanted.

Which I didn't.

"How about instead of an eagle, you do a portrait of George Clooney. That way, when I'm taking the garbage out, I can at least having something purty to look at along the way."

"I'm not sure we can do George Clooney," Todd said.

"Don't be ridiculous, Todd. Only a crazy woman would want an eight-foot circular portrait of George Clooney on her patio. What I meant to say was Taye Diggs. I mean, how hard can this be? You can take a picture of anybody to the bakery and they can form a perfect likeness in ten different colors of spun sugar in under an hour and you can't give me Matthew Fox's image on one lousy cobblestone patio?"

"Well," Todd said, "we have seagulls, too. Some people think those are nice."

Oh, just forget it. I'm banking on all the attention being focused on that mulched chili pepper anyhow.

6

Install Your Dishwasher?
"Ottydidit"

❦

With our kitchen project slowly morphing into a kitchen/laundry room/office nook/complete landscape redesign project, long gone was the notion that we might actually come in "under budget."

To even write those words now, and to remember uttering them aloud, is to confess to being only slightly more intelligent than sweater fuzz.

"The way things are going," I had told hubby while looking at my Wal-Mart calculator, "it looks as if we may actually have money left over!"

Yes, there was much rejoicing in the land as we recalled all the "friends" who had said, almost eagerly, "Ha! Kitchen re-do, eh? Just write down your budget and then, what? Oh, yeah. Set it on fire! You always run over, maybe double or triple. You'd do better to use that budget of yours to wipe your ass. That way you'd get at least a little use out of it."

What would the naysayers say now? According to the calculator, we were doing just fine.

So we forgot the plumbing.

It's overrated, really, that whole continuous flow of water coming out of the faucets thing.

Oh, and the appliances. I mean with all the demolition going on, it's not like we were thinking clearly. The old stove and fridge had long ago been carted off to charity, which tried to cart it back but we pretended we weren't home.

God, what is it with these charitable organizations that expect you to give away perfectly good stuff. Duh, if it worked, we wouldn't be giving it away, now would we?

Anywho, we had no plumbing, so that was the first order of business.

Naturally, the D-Boyz had friends who knew a lot about plumbing and they would basically work for meth.

OK, that's not true, but let's just say that their estimate came in quite a bit lower than anyone else's. It was like Wal-Mart. Sure, you worry if you're getting the same quality but, ultimately, if it saves you money, you're going to put aside that nagging notion that you just bought a calculator made by a tiny Malaysian embryo who was paid a nickel an hour, 'cause, at heart, you're cheap.

Our plumbers consisted of a man known as Daddy Lloyd, who looked a lot like Santa and was twice as nice, his sons, and assorted sons-in-law and live-in boyfriends.

"Lloyd's Boyz" showed up every morning in a battered bus that was so old it looked like its previous owner had been Moses.

On the first morning, Dion took me aside to explain something about Lloyd's Boyz.

"They have their own language," he said. "It's hard to understand 'em so just nod your head a lot and leave 'em the hell alone. They know what they're doing."

At first, I was sure Dion was exaggerating. I was getting used to the occasional stretching of the truth. One short term carpenter had claimed he'd have to knock off early on account of he had "severed a major artery in my leg," only I found out later that he just wanted to catch Lamb of God at the House of Blues that night.

Besides, how "backward" could these fellas talk, anyway? They all lived within ten miles of my house and a Sharper Image store for heaven's sake. It wasn't like I was Liam Neeson trying to understand Jodie Foster's weird "chickapee" speeches in *Nell*. Nell had learned to talk from the trees and the birds and the bear farts in the woods around her, so naturally she was hard to understand.

Lloyd's boyz were all big and blond and looked utterly capable as they dragged an assortment of plumbing paraphernalia from the innards of the Moses bus.

After about a week of heeding Dion's advice, I started to think that not speaking to Lloyd's boyz was rude and they probably thought I was Snooty Homeowner Lady. The thought of this just hurt my heart, so I decided to make nice.

"Hi there," I said one morning to one of the boyz, who looked exactly like the Brawny towel guy.

"Heydihodimoofy!"

Alrighty then.

Over the next few weeks, like a sort of cultural anthropologist, I hid behind plywood and tried to decode their strange speech. The only word I ever recognized was a perfectly enunciated "Cocksucker!" when one of 'em hit his head on the underside of the sink.

Finally, something I understood and it had been used, I might add, in perfect context.

As the days wore on, I realized the boyz were eloquent cussers, although I was still completely unable to decipher any of their normal speech. It didn't matter; they were plumbing geniuses and they worked, uncomplainingly, under the house and even in the Death by Basement.

This work ethic was thrilling considering that the last plumbers I'd used never showed up on time. Half the time, they couldn't show up because one or all of them had a court date. One said I shouldn't worry because he was going to be using the tried-and-true "toddi defense."

"What's that?" I'd naively asked.

"The other dude did it, get it? Toddi?"

Clever.

Another had—I swear to God—been thrown into jail after taking issue with the judge and revealing the inside of his bottom lip, which had been tattooed rather elegantly with the words "F@#$ You" in *script*. Who needs words when you can let your bottom lip do all the talking?

And even though my current plumbers had some kind of weird version of Tourette's while working, we got along just fine.

I discovered that it's actually not so bad to communicate via obscenities.

I'd point at a leaky faucet and say simply, "Shit."

They'd respond with a slow whistle followed by a wholly sympathetic, "Son of a bitch!"

And then the repair would begin in earnest.

While linguistic snobs would say that cursing is the lowest form of human communication, they'd never had such excellent plumbers in their house.

Realizing that I'd forgotten to tell one of Lloyd's boyz that I'd changed my mind about the location of the pot filler, I just pointed to the hole he'd drilled and said, "Bullshit!"

Wordlessly, he plugged up the hole and went to work on a new spot.

Lloyd, himself, never cursed. A gentle, round man with endless patience, he reminded me of Papa Smurf except for the being blue part. I could understand every word Lloyd said, so he acted as interpreter for some of my more complicated questions that couldn't be resolved with a simple "asshole" or the like. Besides, cussing in front of Lloyd would've been like cussing in front of Billy Graham, which any right-thinking Southerner knows would send you straight to hell.

Occasionally Lloyd would say something in such a bizarre Carolina drawl that I had trouble making it out but, with time, I came to realize that "ottydidit" was Lloydspeak for "I've already completed this particular task" and "swanamonado" meant "this is something I am planning to do in the future."

Once the kitchen was plumbed, it was time to buy new appliances.

I had my heart set on stainless steel because that's what they always put in those poor people's houses on *Extreme Makover: Home Edition* and, well, if it's good enough for the man with no arms and his dwarf wife and their eighteen adopted special-needs children, it's sure as hell good enough for me.

An acquaintance that was also going through a kitchen renovation asked how mine was proceeding and I told her I was finally at the appliance-shopping stage.

"Me, too," she said. "I'm not going to do that stupid stainless, though. That is *so* yesterday. What are you going to pick?"

"Oh," I said, kind of enjoying how crappy she was going to feel in a few seconds, "stupid stainless."

"Oh."

While she squirmed like a worm in hot ashes, I told her not to apologize anymore, that everybody's different and that's what makes this country truly great.

That and Ty Pennington, who is just so adorable in a vacant, puka-shell-necklace-wearing kind of way that it makes you want to cut off a few of your appendages just to meet him.

Almost.

7

Stainless Is a Steal Thanks to Cutiepie Salesman

❧

Appliance shopping for the "stupid stainless" proved to be downright educational. I've always been the kind of shopper who buys the mid-priced model, and that was my strategy this time as I set out to select a new stove and refrigerator.

In the appliance store, I met my new best friend, whom I'll call "Cutiepie," because he was, and more importantly because he got fired later on for giving away too many great bargains and I don't want to be sued.

My friend Amy had advised me to visit "Cutiepie" because

she had basically walked out of the store with a huge stupid stainless refrigerator of her own a few weeks earlier and had ended up paying about 300 bucks.

"How is this possible?" I said, opening and closing the doors to her new fridge and marveling at the fingerprint-resistant surface.

"It just is," she said. "Just wait and see."

I asked for Cutiepie by name at the store and he hurried over as soon as he finished helping another couple, who were yelping and high-fiving one another. This seemed like a very good sign; most shoppers don't get all that emotional when they buy a dishwasher.

"I heard that you, uh, really discount stuff," I said to Cutiepie. I spoke in a hushed tone as if I were asking Paulie Walnuts to off somebody for me and bury the mutilated remains in the Pine Barrens.

"Do you know what you want yet?"

"Yep, that twenty-eight-cubic-foot over there with the French doors and the bottom freezer."

"Whoa," Cutiepie said. "You're talking mucho dinero for that baby."

"I know, but," and I lowered my voice again, "I heard that you were really good at wheeling and dealing."

Next thing I know, there is a nearly invisible scrape on the side of "my" refrigerator. I almost didn't see the Swiss Army knife drop softly back into the pocket of Cutiepie's leather jacket.

"Wow," said Cutiepie. "Now how the hell did that happen? I'm gonna have to discount that. How does $950 sound?"

"Perfect," I said, fondling the tempered glass vegetable bins inside my new very slightly damaged fridge.

"What kind of stove are you looking for?" Cutiepie asked.

"Dual fuel," I said, having done a ridiculous amount of obsessive-compulsive homework on the subject. Sure, this was more top-end than mid-price, but I'd saved so much on the fridge, I was feeling kind of flush.

"Those aren't cheap," Cutiepie said again, sagely, but with the corners of his mouth going up a bit even as he spoke.

"I know, I know. But I have my heart set on the gas cooktop and the electric convection range. I liked the one I saw over . . . there!"

"You mean the one that was damaged in shipment?"

"Huh? No."

Cutiepie rolled his big blue eyes and sighed. Play along, lady, the gesture said.

"Oh! Right! Yes, that one. That's the one. It's so horribly damaged, I imagine I'll be entitled to a substantial discount."

"You bet," said Cutiepie, punching a bunch of numbers into a computer.

"Hey! Looks like you qualify for an instant rebate today," he said.

I so wanted to have this man-boy's children.

The thrills kept coming in the form of free delivery "just because."

When the delivery truck lumbered onto my street a few weeks later, there was an "accident" with the hand truck and the delivery guy cheerfully knocked another $150 off the price of the stove.

"But I can't even see any damage," I protested. After all, I'm not a crook.

"Lady, there's a dent right there."

And there it was. About the size of my pinky toenail and it wouldn't even show once the stove was dropped between the base cabinets.

He tossed me a basket full of stupid stainless fingerprint remover and some other freebies that Cutiepie had thought I might enjoy.

A few weeks later, after the stove at my parents' condo up and died, I told them not to fret.

"I have a friend," I said very mysteriously. "And he can get us a really good price on a stove. Don't worry; just let me handle it."

"Why are you whispering?" my mother asked. "Is this friend of yours some kind of crook or something? I don't want a stolen stove. None of that fell-off-the-back-of-a-truck stuff. Do you know what they do to old people in jail? No? I don't either, but I'll bet they'll make your father pretend to be somebody's girlfriend and that will just kill him, if the slop they call food doesn't get him first."

Well. If you watch twenty episodes of *Law & Order* on cable every week, this is what happens. My friend, Tricia, actually has it worse. On a recent visit to her mother, she found the sweet ol' thing blowing her nose into a Bounty towel, devastated that the nice doctor-lady visiting Dodge City had died from tetanus on *Gunsmoke*. And my friend Rae's mama watches so much TV that, when the phone rings, she grabs the remote and screams "Hello! Hello! Who's there?" into it. "Damned telemarketers," she usually says before tossing it back to the side and resuming her weekly afternoon obsession with *Little House on the Prairie*.

"That little girl is so sad being blind and all," says Rae's mama. "She's got that good-looking husband and she can't even see him. He might as well look like Osama."

It took a little while, but I finally convinced my parents that Cutiepie was legit; he just knew that, sometimes, those nicks and dings can really save you money.

I walked into the appliance store with a bounce in my step and asked a less dreamy salesclerk if Cutiepie was working.

"Him? Heck no. He was giving the whole store away. People come in here and ask for him all the time. What? Did he sell you a front-loading washer and dryer for fifty bucks?"

"No! That's crazy," I said, silently pouting that I had missed out on one of his patented bargains.

"We're still digging out from this guy's 'generosity,'" said the less dreamy guy, who was now starting to solidly resemble a toad.

When he asked how he could help me today, I just shrugged.

"My parents need a new kitchen stove. Electric. Nothing too fancy because they don't like a lot of gizmos, Greatest

Generation, you know. They'll wipe down and reuse a piece of Saran Wrap until it's the size of a disposable contact lens."

He showed me a nice basic white stove that had a big yellow tag attached to it: "$725.00" it read.

Toad Boy insisted on reading from the owner's manual for several minutes reciting a list of the stove's qualities, high-lighted by its ability to "cook food."

"Oh," I said. "You mean it's not a time machine?"

Toad Boy wasn't amused.

"How much?" I asked.

"The price is right there," he said. "It's $725."

"Yes, I can see that, but surely there's a little flex room. No-body ever pays the price listed."

"Sure they do," he said. "This isn't a car you can haggle over; it's a stove and this one is $725. Plus tax. And delivery."

"You look like a toad," I blurted.

"What?"

"Nothing. I said, I gotta hit the road. I'll take it."

As he rang me up and got delivery directions, he made a pitch for buying the extended warranty for another $150.

"If something goes wrong, you're covered," Toad Boy said, adding in a halting telemarketer voice: "Don't you think that $150 is a small price to pay for that kind of peace of mind?"

At this point, I felt what could only be described as a physi-cal ache for Cutiepie.

"You mean you think that this stove is going to fall apart in a year? What kind of piece of crap is this?"

"No, that's not what I meant," said Toad Boy. "It's for your protection is all. Plus, if I sell eight more of these warranties in the next three days, I'll win a trip to the Bahamas. Uh-oh. Did I just say that out loud?"

"Yep," I said.

"Oh."

The last big-ticket purchase was a new hot water heater, which turned out to be another adventure.

Because of the configuration of our newly created laundry room, there was no room for one of the round, traditional water heaters, so we would have to buy the energy-efficient eco-friendly peacenik one that provides hot water on demand.

The good news was that I am very demanding when it comes to hot water and pretty much everything else. The bad news was that it was horribly expensive.

"It'll pay for itself the first two years," said Jim, my kitchen designer and project manager, who looks exactly like a cross between Jesus and Tom Cruise, I kid you not.

"But it's so much," I whined to Jim one morning as Lloyd's boyz waited for my decision, cursing continuously.

"Is this one of those times where I just need to stand here and remind you how much I look like Jesus and Tom Cruise and you just finally give in and do what I say?"

He was awfully good at that, Jim was. He had those same piercing blue Jesus-eyes that looked just like the blind girl on *Little House*, now that I thought of it.

Finally, I called around and asked friends and family what they thought about this. Every one of them said this hot water heater was the wave of the future.

"Paul Harvey always advertises it," said my mother.

"I thought he was dead."

"I know," she said, solemnly. "Everybody thinks that."

Most people reminded me that you get a huge break on your taxes when you buy this thing. It's like the Prius of hot water heaters. Ed Begley Jr. would try to drive it if he could.

Whatever. I'm not one of those earthy types. I think organic produce looks nasty and I like my meat to be injected with stuff that makes it pretty and shiny in the grocery store counter. I like my chickens fat and full of synthetically produced hormones instead of those pale, gimpy little free-range things that wouldn't fill a hollow tooth.

But, even more than that, I just like never, ever running out of hot water. I'd buy this thing again even if it meant I had to shower *with* Paul Harvey every night. Dead or alive.

8

Screw the Tsunamis; I Got a Kitchen to Pay For

With the kitchen nearly completed, hubby and I revisited the budget for the eleventy-hundredth time. But first, we strolled through the room, hand in hand, admiring the result of months of hard work. The room was gorgeous and I looked forward to heating various Hormel microwaveable entrees in it for many happy years to come.

The team was tickled, too. Jim/Jesus/Tom Cruise was thrilled. Lloyd's boyz and Dion's boyz were all whistling and the cursing had almost disappeared. Trucks were being packed up for the last time and cigarette butts were being raked up like leaf piles. We even put them in those jack-o-lantern lawn and leaf bags that you use to decorate your redneck yard in October.

Not exactly as wholesome as pine straw but spooky in its own way.

Unexpectedly, a twinge of separation anxiety set in when it was time to say good-bye and write the last check.

I'd already had Lloyd stay to fix an imaginary squeak in the garbage disposal. But this was silly; it was time to take my home back. Yes, my hons, it was time to cut the cord.

And wrap it around my neck. As we totaled the amount of the job, hubby and I stared at one another in disbelief. Or maybe we were both thinking the same thing: Whoa. I need to take out a *much* bigger life insurance policy on you.

Kidding! Only someone speeding on the highway to Crazy Town would think like that. But we did need to take a serious look at our shrunken finances.

We'd spent our savings and then some. Now we'd need to stumble into some serious cash. Either that, or I'd be forced to—ohmigod—go back to work.

As in the kind of work that I hadn't done for years, the kind that requires pantyhose and minty-fresh breath and perky demeanor even when the troll sitting in the next cubicle is making your life miserable by eating smelly canned beef stew at her desk.

I shuddered to think about leaving my little home office. I'd been up here, like Rapunzel in her tower except for the fact that I have really crappy hair, writing and ruminating at my own pace for the past eight years. To tell the truth, life on Planet Celia had been pretty swell.

Clearly, going back to work for The Man couldn't happen. Nope, it was going to be up to hubby to make money quick. But how?

Finally, it hit me. He could step up and tell the world, or at least the readership of *Us* magazine, that *he* was the real father of poor, dead Anna Nicole Smith's baby. (This was pre-Birkhead, you must remember.)

At the rate men were signing up to claim daddyhood (and, not coincidentally, a share of baby Dannielynn's potential gazillion dollar inheritance), I figured hubby would come in behind Urkel and slightly ahead of Donald Trump on the sign-up sheets.

Everybody knew Trump would say he was the daddy at some point. I waited for the press conference when he'd say: "This baby has been fathered by the most handsome and charismatic producer and star of the most exciting reality show that has ever been shown in the history of television. And that includes your high-definition, your plasma, and your just plain television."

The way things were going at the time, I halfway expected poor Britney Spears, in a desperate attempt to attract attention to something other than her world-weary cooter, to say *she* was the baby's father.

I was surprised that K-Fed, that greasy white-boy rapper in the wife-beater, didn't step up to claim to be the baby-daddy. He ain't much to look at but he has a supernatural ability to induce pregnancy.

In general, I believe that anytime there is a question of paternity, in the United States or abroad, K-Fed should be hauled in and swabbed.

Hubby balked at signing up, pointing out with his typical "man logic" that he had never even met Anna Nicole Smith, much less impregnated her.

Details.

You didn't see that stopping Rosie O'Donnell, who I fully expected to claim to be the daddy because, let's face it, she's twice the man of any of the other candidates. She's definitely more of a man than Arnold Schwarzenegger, who vehemently denied that he was the baby's father because he was "having to run Cally-fawn-ee-ya's government and t'ings of t'at nature."

"Look," I told hubby, "even that fossil that's married to Zsa Zsa Gabor is claiming to be the daddy, and you can look at him and tell he's shootin' blanks."

Hubby continued to balk at the idea, but I pointed out that if enough folks muddied the DNA waters, it could turn into a class-action suit and he could be one of hundreds, perhaps thousands, to get a piece of the Dannielynn pie.

Mercenary? Perhaps, but y'all know that with me it's always family first.

In the meantime, I had a book to promote, which meant I was going to be away from home, and my gorgeous new kitchen, for more than a month. I love book tours because I don't have to cook or clean or convince my kid I know jack shit about the square root of 1,342.

In Dallas, I got to stay in the same hotel as Cyndi Lauper.

She just wanted to have fun and I was like, "Cyndi, give it a rest! I really have to answer my E-mails." OK, I didn't actually meet her but she was on my floor.

This hotel was Zen-influenced and the TV had four separate relaxation and yoga channels but no HBO. This did nothing to relax me. It also had a restaurant where I ordered—swear to God—an eighteen-dollar bowl of oatmeal for breakfast.

The waiter said, "Ahhh, an excellent choice" and I laughed really hard and said, "Dude. It's *oatmeal*."

He had the last laugh, though, because this oatmeal must have had crack, in it. It was the best oatmeal on the planet.

Unfortunately, the month my book came out was the same month that Everyone in the Free World had a book come out.

It seemed like everyone was writing about (A) dogs or (B) heaven or (C) dogs in heaven. All of them were crowding onto my rightful place on the bestseller list. In one town, I arrived one night after a standing-room-only crowd showed up for Fannie Flagg, a great Southern writer-chick who had written a bestseller about, yes, heaven. The bookstore owner went on and on about how they'd had everybody dress in white for the signing and they had uplighting in the trees and served tiny white tea cakes.

What would I get, I wondered. A bag of Combos and a single naked bulb?

It could be worse, I thought, as I checked into a luscious hotel near Mobile. I could be James Frey.

The truth was, ever since Frey got caught embellishing his hugely successful druggie memoir, *A Million Little Pieces*, I'd been thinking I should do the same thing. That was before Oprah took him to the metaphorical woodshed of course.

Yes, before that, Frey was riding high. Literally. But somebody told somebody and they told somebody else that there was no way all that shit could happen to one dude.

Frey got dragged onto *Larry King Live* and admitted, with his precious mama at his side, that he might have exaggerated some of the more disturbing and law-breaking parts of the book.

His bad.

Even as I watched him squirm, I realized that a made-up memoir might be my ticket to not just paying for the kitchen, but adding a pool. There was plenty of room in the backyard of my money pit after all. We could even put up a fence to keep the neighbors from pretending to drown and then suing us.

Frey's enormous success inspired me not to settle for a truthful memoir, recounting an ordinary upbringing in a small but boring Southern town, but to reach out and confess to things that I may not have exactly done but, perhaps, once watched on TV or saw in the movies.

Like the time I robbed a convenience store and shot a man in Reno, just to watch him die. Er, sorry. That was a Johnny Cash song. Cash, now that I think about it, also was accused of manufacturing his lawless "man in black" image. He never served time in Folsom Prison but he didn't exactly discourage the impression when fans bought millions of copies of *Folsom Prison Blues*. Which seriously rocks, by the way.

Clearly, it would be better to write a memoir that had less truth and more crime.

Frey's drug rehab book was powerful, life-changing and, oh yes, made up. But powerful nonetheless.

But no more powerful, ladies and gentlemen, than the riveting true-life account of a small-town Southern humor writer who kept Elvis hidden beneath her bed for more than two decades!

That's right. I'm going to call it *A Million Little Nanner Sandwiches* and then I'm going to go on *Oprah* and make more money than God or Rachael Ray, who is probably already at work on her next bestseller: *Rachael Ray Makes Dog Sandwiches! In Heaven!*

Back in Dallas, I decided to make the pilgrimage to the mothership that is Neiman Marcus, where I accidentally spent forty-eight dollars on a brow pencil. For a Maybelline girl from way back, this was downright guilt-inducing. Still, I deserved it. I was staying in a hotel where I was—I swear—the only guest not affiliated with a national cheerleading convention.

If you ever want to feel old, just ride an elevator with thirty-five giggling teens wearing their hair in buns of sponge-rubber rollers and saying "Shut *up*!" a lot to each other.

These girls were Mean Girls, just like in the movie. When I asked them to let me off because it was my floor, they eyed me from the top of my velour jogging suit to the bottom and visibly snarled. I was something sticky on the bottom of a Payless shoe.

"What*ever*," they said, nearly in unison.

Later on, I saw a couple of them in Neiman's and was rewarded by this delicious conversation between two cheerleaders that I'll call Posh and Paris.

Posh: "Ohmigod, this Prada purse is so cute. I am so going to buy this in every color. My mom is so going to like so totally flip out."

Paris: "Ohmigod, you really shouldn't do that." (She said this with that upward inflection that all these girls use when they talk, as though every statement is actually a question? It's so incredibly irritating that it makes me want to strangle them?)

Posh: "Ohmigod, why not, bee-atch?"

Paris: "Because you should, like, use some of that money to help, like, the Tsunamis?"

Posh: "The who?"

Paris: "The Tsunamis. They were on the news. People are sending them money?"

Posh: "Ohmigod, you are so random."

Paris: (giggling) "I know?"

Yes, I thought to myself as I pondered Paris' developing social consciousness. They are a proud people, those Tsunamis. We really can't do enough for 'em.

9

Taxing Matters (IRS Means I'm Really Stressed)

When you're self-employed like me, you have to worry about really boring things like making quarterly estimated tax payments. Are you asleep yet?

I have a hard time remembering this "law," so every year, along about April fifteenth, I begin to slowly and carefully freak out.

It's about this same time of year that it dawns on me: We could save a lot of money by doing our own taxes.

Why shouldn't we, after all? Would you go to a "doctor" to fix your broken arm? You would? Wuss.

I mean it's our income. Who is more uniquely qualified to deduct the new gas grill and tiki torches as business expenses?

Besides, how hard can it be to do your own taxes? All you need is a smidgen of patience, a freshly sharpened pencil, and a handy supply of Schedule 2 narcotics, right?

It might not have been the best idea to do my own taxes during the year of the remodel. For starters, I had no idea how to claim the tax credit for the amazing Paul Harvey water heater or a bunch of other stuff we'd done that was supposed to qualify for some sort of historic district exemption.

But I was still confident that, between hubby and I, we'd figure it out.

All we needed to get started was the appropriate forms.

Here's the good news: The IRS is seriously trying to become more user-friendly. It wants us to like them so much that it smacks of desperation. The IRS is like the awkward teen that yearns to sit at the cool table in the lunchroom but knows she never will because she doesn't have enough money or isn't smart enough or doesn't really think that the band Yes is all that and a bucket of chicken. Oh, sorry. Having a little flashback to '74 there.

Anyway, I'd seen all sorts of ads about the IRS' willingness to help out. First stop: the shiny new local office for forms and guidance.

I walked into a cavernous space, the carpet so new that you couldn't help but notice the overwhelming aroma of potentially carcinogenic carpet fibers. The place reeked of new paint and just-opened office supplies. It was, honestly, a vision, right on down to the several *hundred* padded chairs that had been perfectly arranged in long, straight rows that would do an obsessive-compulsive proud.

I was very impressed. Also puzzled. Because there wasn't a single human being in this enormous room, just a row of walled cubicles as far as the eye could see.

"Hello!" I called, my voice echoing back to me. Cool. I did it again.

Finally, a voice came from behind one of the far cubicles.

"Please take a number."

OK, for some reason this struck me as hilarious. I mean there was *no one* within ten miles of this room. But this is the IRS and it can't help its nerdy self. Instead of just saying, "C'mon back," I gotta take a number.

OK, I'll play.

With number in hand, I sat. And sat. Finally, a few minutes into the process, with only the sound of the air conditioning to keep me company, I got the silly church giggles and laughed so hard that my palms sweated all over my number, which was 100, by the way.

Finally, after a few more minutes, I heard the disembodied voice of the IRS agent call out stiffly: "NUMBER 100."

I said to the empty room: "I think that's me!"

I walked way down to greet "the voice," which turned out to belong to a very nice and helpful woman. She told me, among other things, I would need Form 1040-ES, which would contain coupons.

"That's great!" I said, instantly warming to the U.S. government. "For like Arby's or Domino's or something. Hey. I don't want to be ungrateful but if you've got one for Pizza Hut that would be even better because they're doing that thing again where they fill the crust full of cheese and you just pop off these little heavenly bites of warm cheese dough."

She stared at me, uncomprehending.

"That's very funny," she said, without a trace of a smile. "These are coupons to accompany your estimated tax payments."

"Oh," I said, irrationally disappointed that there would be no cents-off on Buffalo wings.

She then handed me a customer satisfaction survey but all the admonitions to fill in the bubbles exactly and precisely and LEAVE NO STRAY MARKS were too intimidating.

Face it, IRS. Until you learn to loosen up a little, you're never going to sit at the cool table.

Fast-forward a few weeks and you find me sitting on the floor, surrounded by tiny scraps of paper, booklets of rules and advice, unable to complete my own taxes and, frankly, at this point, bathe myself.

Hubby took pity on me and started reading through some of the helpful IRS literature.

"We need to do more for charity," he said. "Oh, and have eleven more children."

Great. The charity thing wasn't a bad idea except the IRS was persnickety about what kind of charity. For the first eight months of the year, you could claim 40.5 cents per business mile and fourteen cents a mile for any driving related to charity but you would get twenty-nine cents a mile for charity related to Hurricane Katrina.

During the last three months of the year you could get thirty-four cents a mile for Katrina-related charity and 48.5 cents a mile for business.

I am not making this up.

We wondered if simply discussing the awful hurricane in the car while driving would count. Hubby and I began to interject statements about Katrina everywhere we went, but it didn't feel right.

Charity, as it turned out, could really help us out. In my case, I decided that it would be charitable of me to volunteer more at my kid's elementary school. After all, I could deduct the hours I spent there and even the drive there and back.

But I wasn't really the kind of mom who was good at the crafty stuff. Last year, when I was asked to make marshmallow "monsters" for the Halloween carnival, they'd burned and exploded and looked just like the fat guy on *Lost* with chow mein noodles sticking out of his sides.

Nope, I would have to play to my strengths. Fortunately, right about then, an opening came up for an advisor for the school newspaper. Perfect.

Two decades in the newspaper business had surely equipped me for something besides listening to people carp about how the print is getting smaller. Oh, sorry. That was me.

I began my "charity volunteer tax-saving newspaper work" immediately, with a staff meeting where I met the twenty-two fresh-faced members of the school newspaper staff, all in grades three through five.

In some ways, it was just like old times in the newsroom. Except I don't recall ever having to stop a budget meeting to ask one of the reporters to "please stop turning your ears inside out." On the other hand, well, wow.

Overall, the first "charity tax-saving meeting" wasn't all that different from the "real" newspaper meetings of my past. A couple of reporters flirted with each other and had no new ideas; another refused to share a byline on the new principal story; another admitted he hadn't even started the interviews on a story due in two days; at least six showed up with no pencil or paper. Yes, it was very much like old times only everybody was shorter and better dressed.

Even though I wasn't being paid, I enjoyed it immensely. The kid-reporters asked great questions. One was doing a story on the death of the school science lab's ancient chinchilla. It was a real tear-jerker and she'd even gotten a picture.

"Is it OK that even though he's technically dead, he's alive in this picture?" she asked.

"Of course," I said. "Let's remember him as he was, a big, fat, furry rodent that fathered more offspring than Mel Gibson."

"Huh?"

"No dead animal pictures, sweetie."

"Right, chief!" she said.

This was so much fun, I wanted to pay them for letting me do it! I was so ripping off the government with these "charitable" hours.

Next up was an earnest young man needing help with his new-teacher-profile questions.

I looked them over and had to laugh at No. 5: "Are you married? If not, why not?"

Probably the only real difference between the newsrooms was that, in this one, I was the only one drinking coffee. I resolved to do something about that the next week.

"Could I have decaf?" asked the smart Indian girl.

"Well, duh, that would kind of defeat the point, now wouldn't it, Syri?"

"It's Sneha."

"Whatever."

With charitable "work" to deduct, we just had to get busy on those additional eleven children. Gawd, where was K-Fed when you really needed him?

Look, I hate to belabor the point but the man is a baby-making machine. I envision dozens of female baristas finding themselves inexplicably pregnant mere moments after serving K-Fed his double-whammy-hotsie-totsie mocha latte with a shot of Boone's Farm Strawberry to go. He's like the superhero of impregnation. As women around the globe pat their tummies and smile gratefully toward the tiny corn-rowed wonder growing within, K-Fed has, like Steve Martin discovering sex in *The Jerk*, finally found his "special purpose."

Age wasn't on my side though. And it seemed that the IRS was changing its mind daily about the "true definition of a child."

I define a child as the height-challenged person living in

your home that eats all your Toaster Strudels, *even the ones you hid behind the bag of chicken livers,* and reprograms your phone to ring "SexyBack" while you're not looking.

But no! The IRS definition of a child changed from code section to code section until there was so much complaining that, in an unprecedented showing of common sense, they decided to go with the Toaster Strudel definition after all.

With volunteer "charity" work under way and a "child" at home, I began to think that I could pull off this whole tax thing and maybe even get a refund.

Dreema Fay, my tech-savvy friend and Web designer, reminded me that I should be sure to document all the costs of maintaining my Web site.

Dreema Fay knows I don't like talking about computer things. Technology alternately fascinates and repels me. It's that familiar push-pull of emotions that you feel while watching a Discovery Channel show where the bunny rabbit becomes some snake's McLunch or seeing photographs of Tori Spelling's second wedding.

That said, I'm grateful beyond words for Al Gore's Internet invention not only because it makes research for my "work" so easy but also because where else can you learn, via forwarded E-mail, if you boil a Western omelette in a Ziploc bag, it turns out perfect every time?

Knowledge is power, y'all.

Dreema Fay offered to come over and walk me through Turd-O Tax but I resisted. She knows when it comes to computers, I have an attention span shorter than the line on opening night of the latest Rob Schneider movie.

"No, no," I told her on the phone one day. "I've got this tax thing down. We're going to get back a bundle what with all my charity work, Katrina."

"You mean Dreema," she said.

"Right. But see if I can mention the word 'Katrina' during every phone call, I can deduct the time I spent talking to you. Katrina."

"That's sick and illegal," said Dreema Fay.

Perhaps to get even with me, Dreema/Katrina sent me an E-mail later that day listing all the search terms that route people to my Web site. They included: "preschool diseases," "books about rocks," "girls making doody" (I know, that one scares me, too), "Oprah wears a watch," "Teri Hatcher should shut up," and my personal favorite: "Osmond butt cheeks."

While I do recall writing about the Chiclet-toothed singing Mormons several years ago, I can assure you that they are, and were, too wholesome to even possess butt cheeks.

Curiouser still was how someone landed at my site by simply typing in the words "rectal region rash."

And, yes, I'm trying not to take that one personally.

Truthfully, after many tense weeks spent trying to decipher the wacky IRS rules, I'd prefer a rectal region rash to ever doing my own taxes again.

Let someone else be Number 100 next year.

Part 11

❧ Just Kid-ding ❦

10

Harry Potter Bitch-slaps Nancy Drew

W̲hile I'm all in favor of encouraging children to read, read, read, I don't see why it always has to be Harry Potter.

Sure, plucky welfare mom J.K. Rowling scribbled her first book in a dank Scottish coffee shop whilst her precious baby napped in a stroller beside her dreaming of a life without coal gray skies, but enough!

And whither the baby-daddy? If J.K. Rowling had been a Southern mama, she wouldn't have been hunched over her writing pad, trying to make enough money to never again tell the waiter, "I'll just have the haggis." She'd have his triflin' ass in court, making sure that he was doing his daddy duty. On the other hand, if she'd married a proper Southern gentleman, J.K. might not have had the "wolf at the door" mentality while she wrote.

When you've got a husband who works a job, like me, you tend to put off writing projects in favor of trips to the mall "just because" and maintaining your winter spray tan.

Kids are wild about Harry and, in my daughter's case, they don't want to read anything else.

Sophie can spend hours discussing all things Dumbledore, Voldemort and Syrius Black. Because I have no idea what she's talking about, she dismisses me as a "Muggle," which I'm fairly certain isn't Potterspeak for "Fantastic, Perfect Mommy."

I just naturally assumed Soph would be reading Nancy Drew, just as I did at her age. Wrong, Hogwarts-breath. My kid is bored senseless by the wholesome adventures of the "athletic blond girl detective." I suppose after reading about Harry and best friend Ron squaring off against ten-foot-tall furry black spiders inside a cave, the antics that ensue when you return a stolen locket to its rightful owner in the nursing home isn't really that big a deal.

But I still think young readers are missing a great series when they skip Nancy. Who can forget how best gal-pals George and Bess helped her solve *The Secret of the Old Clock?* fueled only by kindly housekeeper Hannah Gruen's yummy lemon bars?

Or how handsome widower father, attorney Carson Drew, encouraged Nancy to follow her detective dreams? Or how her Ken-doll boyfriend, the alliterative Ned Nickerson, offered relaxing rides in his "roadster" for the gang at the end of every solved mystery? Or how everybody used "sleuthing" as a verb without cracking up?

No, no. Sophie will have none of that, preferring instead to read about games played in the air with flying brooms and followed by the drinking of dragon's bile.

She speaks with great authority about Harry's school, where magic is taught to the residents of "dorms" named Gryffindor, Ravenclaw, Hufflepuff, and Slytherin, hardly the kind of names one might see on the "Hello" tags at alumni fund-raisers.

My abysmal lack of interest in Harry Potter means that while Sophie can recite the intricacies of the plots in each book, all I can come up with is a bright smile and a "That Daniel Radcliffe guy is actually pretty hot." To which she just rolls her eyes and looks as if she'd like to turn me into a teapot or toad.

Of course the whole world has Harry Potter fever. Although there is talk that Rowling will eventually kill our boy off, I'm pretty sure she won't be able to walk away from the vast mounds of cash generated by this franchise, although she may tire a bit of all the dark arts stuff. We'll know she's getting weary when we read, sometime in 2010, *Harry Potter Goes Shopping at Wal-Mart and Buys a Coat Made in Cambodia.*

Rowling, with her pre-orders in the millions and her fancy midnight release parties, is hot stuff but there was a time—oh, yes sirree Bob!—when the name of Nancy Drew author Mildred Wirt Benson was on everyone's lips. OK, not really.

The truth is, if I don't start reading, and liking, Harry Potter, I might as well be wearing an invisibility cloak around here. As Nancy would earnestly say, while adjusting her woolen tam, "Criminy!"

Soph and her friends are so into Harry Potter books that they actually spend time trying to write their own little books along similar themes.

This enthusiasm for writing at such an early age is downright shocking but, not to worry, the Scary and Over-Hyped State Writing Test for all fourth-graders should successfully quash the joy for the kids and, mercifully, book-writing can be left to the grown-ups who have, like, mortgages to pay and shit.

Writing has become a big focus ever since President Bush decided to prevail upon Congress to pass the "It Ain't Right to Leave No Child Behind" law, which, mercifully, Laura Bush, being a former librarian *and* being completely made of wax, was able to make sound more smarter.

Before the Big Ooga Booga Scare the Pee Out of You State Writing Test, parents are told what to expect in a helpful "handout" that is sent home in their kid's backpack, which means that it will most likely have a few moist Skittles stuck to it.

OK, here's the sad truth: I've read the Skittle-soaked handout, like, eight times and I still don't understand it. This means that either: (A) I have the brains of hamster dander, or (B) This thing really makes no sense.

The not-so-catchy title, "Classroom Assessment Analytic Rubric," was the first stopper.

I have no idea what a rubric is. Maybe it has something to do with a Rubric's Cube, but what would an obscure toy from the '80s have to do with writing? Yeah, I know it's not spelled the same. So Sioux me.

The funniest part of the handout was the notion that parents are supposed to help "coach" their kids to make sure they don't blow it on the test by using sentence fragments, run-on sentences, or other no-nos. Or as I like to say when I'm feeling particularly writerly, no's-no.

Being a Southern mama, I have to tell y'all that, right away, I sniffed a geographic bias in the test and here's why.

This example was given for using a word the wrong way: "Pete wanted to sale the boat."

Well, maybe that's wrong; maybe not. If Pete is a Southern boy, he might not want to "sail" the boat as the snooty test-writers assume. He might want to fix up that rusty-ass john boat behind Paw-Paw and Mimi's shed and "sell" the boat. In the South, we pronounce that "sale," so there should be some consideration of that. I think.

It's also important, according to the "rubric," to use pronouns correctly on the "I Shit Myself These Questions Are So Hard" writing test.

The example of using a pronoun incorrectly was: "John and myself went to school." They didn't give a reason for why this was wrong so I can only assume if a fourth-grader ever said that sentence to another fourth-grader, he'd get the crap beat out of him for being uppity, the kind of kid who would brag about getting to sale his boat for big money.

Another frequent writing test pitfall, it turns out, is something called "incorrect formulations."

Who that, you say?

The examples included words such as "hisself, theirselves and bestest." Well, that's just about the worstest idea I ever heard of. I *love* those words. Again, I smell the faint odor of geographical snobbery.

What right-thinking Southern child has never uttered the word "hisself," as in "Billy Ray caught hisself on the barbed wire trying to get away from that bull"?

There is simply no acceptable substitute.

Because it wasn't mentioned on the fancy-pants rubric, I'm hoping that the test will allow repeated use of another favorite Southernism: "theyselves," which, of course, is the pluperfect plural subjunctive of the verb "they." An example of correct usage would be: "They saw theyselves on *Cops* and weren't even embarrassed about it."

I told Soph I'd help her study for the Test That Can Literally Stop Your Heart. But I told her to remember: If she doesn't do well, it "won't" my fault.

At times, I wonder just how much you can really teach someone to write anyway.

A long time ago, I decided that I didn't need any formal "edumacation" as my backwoods neighbor growing up called it.

And so, based on the advice of this albino woman who smoked Salem 100's and peed outdoors, I decided to skip college and leap into newspapering at the age of eighteen.

So, no, I don't have a degree and, as much as I'd like to have one, the whole notion of the work associated with it is as appealing as a Wham! comeback.

I'll pass on the horror of being the oldest student in a roomful of flat-stomached Ambers and guys cute enough to be on *The Hills* calling me "ma'am."

Don't get me wrong. I have the highest regard for the non-traditional (old) students. But I'm too insecure to be the only student in the class who has to leave early, not to fetch the keg, but to rush to the Clinique counter because the moisturizer is on sale and there's a free gift with purchase.

Besides, although many mommies do return to college, I'm basically looking for more, not less, "me time."

I actually look forward to my kid's dental appointments because it's the only time in my life when I'm guaranteed at least thirty minutes of uninterrupted magazine reading.

It's possible that I never had the right stuff for college. I do, after all, have a bit of a mouth on me.

Full disclosure: I did enroll in one college course when I was twenty-five because it was about TV's influence on pop culture. The outline was delicious and the textbook fascinating. At the end of the semester, I ripped open my grade report and saw a "B." I immediately told the prof that he had to be kidding.

"I'm the queen of TV and pop culture," I reminded him. "I know the words to every single episode of *The Andy Griffith*

Show including the disappointing Warren-the-deputy years. I can sing the theme songs to obscure '60s Westerns like *Sugarfoot* and *Cheyenne*."

Sadly, the B stood and matters weren't helped much when I told him he was a pretentious elbow-patched asshole whom I fervently hoped would someday take a very long three-hour cruise. Again with the mouth.

I whistled the melody to *Rawhide* AND *Tombstone Territory* on my way out of the room and into a life that would be devoid of a college degree.

The whole thing leaves me feeling a bit hypocritical as I caution Precious that she has to study hard so she can get into a good college.

"But you didn't go to college and you turned out OK," she says.

"You call this OK?" I shriek. "I should've gone to college! The other night on *Wheel . . . of . . . Fortune!* I missed every single puzzle, even the before and after one, and I always get that one. Remember how I got 'Shaving Cream of the Crop'?"

"Yeah, I remember," said Soph. "You called everybody we know to tell them. But so what? All that was left was the 'm' when you got it. Besides, I don't think college is meant to help you with a game show. Maybe you should read more and watch TV less."

Whaaaa?!?

I made the age-old and oddly annoying gesture people make to indicate that they're talking on an imaginary telephone.

"Hello. Orphanage?" I said a bit too loudly. "Yes, I have a charming fourth-grader here who might like to go live with y'all on account of there's *no frikkin way she's related to me!*"

Soph rolled her eyes and returned to reading the latest exploits of the bespectacled junior wizard.

At night, with thoughts of writing tests and the disappointing lack of college degree swirling through my dreams—along with an oddly erotic dream involving Ned Nickerson and me doing unspeakable things in the back of his roadster—I realized that perhaps I was overreacting out of insecurity.

Weren't there on-line college degrees available for people like me? People who just want the degree without the pesky homework and grading experience and inevitable encounter with the devil's spawn, er, Young Republicans Club?

Perhaps I needed an on-line degree. I Googled some the nation's finer fake universities the very next day and that's when I learned about Trinity Southern.

A little more on-line research revealed that TSU might not be the best place to go to make my dream degree happen. Turns out a deputy attorney general, suspicious of the school's degrees, submitted an application for a doctorate for his six-year-old housecat, "Colby," based on the cat's life experiences.

TSU agreed that Colby Cat sounded like a fine candidate for a Ph.D. but was rewarded for its generous interpretation of life education with a nasty charge of fraud.

Not to worry. I hear there's a very qualified Pomeranian hoping to earn a TSU law degree someday soon.

11

Rugby-Playing Lesbians Torpedo Beach Day

❧

As the parent of a young child, you have to be prepared to handle a variety of situations in life, everything from explaining why the kid can't just sit around all day eating Marshmallow Fluff and watching cartoons ("It's good enough for Daddy") to why Bad Things Happen to Good People to one that's, uh, perhaps a little more unusual. Naturally, I'm speaking of how one handles a gaggle of naked lesbian rugby players making out on a public beach in broad daylight.

What? This hasn't happened to you? Well, aren't you the lucky frikkin' duck. Duh-hubby and I had taken the Princess and her little friend to the beach for the afternoon and just as we were settling in for a remarkably wholesome afternoon at our favorite spot, we couldn't help but notice a reenactment that had nothing to do with the usual ones we get in our small Southern city. No, no. This wasn't the usual pack of obsessed Civil War reenactors who whine if someone shows up in polyster, instead of a 100-percent wool uniform, or didn't make their own eyeglasses by hand.

No, no. This was a reenactment of a familiar scene in the surf in *From Here to Eternity* where lovers grope and fondle and kiss in the breaking surf. It's pretty hot, for an old movie starring dead people.

Apparently the rugby-playing lesbians had seen it a few times and were determined to bring it to a family beach in the middle of a Sunday afternoon.

Now I have nothing against rugby or lesbians. In fact, had it been heterosexual tennis players cavorting mere feet from our SpongeBob beach towels I would have been equally freaked out.

"Mommy, why are those girls kissing?" I heard at my elbow.

"Oh, they're just happy to see one another," I said, looking helplessly to hubby who, by this time, had done what any right-thinking American male would do and pulled his beach chair closer and proceeded to stare, trancelike.

The romping in the surf kicked up a notch as one of the lesbian rugby players emerged without her bathing suit bottom, giggling and sprinting about as if she thought this was Club Med instead of possibly the most uptight Republican beach in seven states.

My jaw dropped, y'all. But I had no idea what to do.

Thank God for a good vacationing Yankee grandma. There are just times when the soft-spoken, magnolia-mouthed approach to uncivilized public behavior just isn't going to get the job done.

The Yankee grandma jumped up, knotted her gray hair into a quick ponytail, lit a cigarette, and stormed into the surf to boldly confront the bottomless lesbians.

"Hey, you guys!" she hollered, each syllable clipped and loud enough to be heard over the noisy waves. "I got my grandkids out here for crap's sake. Knock that nasty shit off before I call the cops uh ready."

Whoa. That sure trumped the half-formed plan in my noggin, namely bribing them to stop and get dressed in exchange for the thirteen-by-nine-inch Pyrex dish full of luscious homemade banana pudding in my cooler.

Southern women generally despise confrontation, particularly with very large, toned women who could snap their necks like a Captain's wafer and laugh at the bloody stump.

And then something amazing happened.

The girls hung their heads and *apologized*. One of them placed her hands over her bidness and said, "My bad."

Well, yes, your bad, missy. And, no offense, but get to a hair removal expert pronto. That thing's gonna block out the sun, bless your heart.

Part of the reason we don't know how to handle things like this in the South is that we're bred to be sweet. We send our children to cotillion classes so that they will know how to behave in society but nobody ever tells us how to confront naked lesbians on a public beach.

Cotillion classes are a big deal in the South. The Princess announced that she wanted to take them a while back but I haven't enrolled her yet.

The truth is, they don't seem all that relevant anymore. There was just something kind of odd about the goals of the cotillion classes being held at our local snootiest country club.

By the end of the six weeks, each child would learn restaurant manners, school etiquette, proper use of silverware, and line dancing.

That's right. Line dancing.

Apparently these days, it is just as important to know how to execute an impeccable electric slide as it is to write a pretend thank-you note to "Peanuts the Polite Elephant."

I hate to quibble here but the elephants I've seen at the circus and in the zoo are anything but polite. They roll around in the mud and stuff straw up their noses.

Still, I didn't want to discourage Sophie. After all, wouldn't it have been wonderful if those rugby lesbians had taken cotillion? I'm not saying we need to raise a generation of Little Lord and Lady Fauntleroy's but, just think, if Paris Hilton had taken cotillion, I'm sure she would've learned that posing for pictures with your tongue down another's larynx is considered distasteful. Ditto crooning crotch-grabber Usher.

But line dancing? What are these little kids supposed to do after they finish the dance? Retire to their tables at the club with Bunny and Sissy and debate the relative merits of their small-, mid-, and large cap holdings?

Still, there was more to like about cotillion than not. The cotillion teacher made the kids recite "When at the store with Mom to shop, I must not run or skip or hop!"

Or, as the Princess did when she was three, loudly announce as we wheeled by the beer and wine aisle that I shouldn't forget my "mommy juice." Thanks ever so.

So yes, I suppose cotillion could teach a few good lessons and the National League of Junior Cotillions seems to be trying to stay relevant. For older students, there's even a class called "Digital Courtesy in Public Places." I'm not sure but I think it means to never give anybody the finger.

There's even a course in sports etiquette. Perhaps Barry Bonds and his size nine hat could teach that one. ("Hey kids! When injecting extract of bull pituitary gland directly into your buttocks, try to avoid unseemly flailing and screaming.")

Raising a proper young woman in the South isn't as easy as it used to be. Apparently, things aren't any better if you're an international star.

Madonna has announced that she won't let her daughter date until she's eighteen.

Of all the moms I expected to have my back on the dating thing, Madonna had to be the least likely. This is the woman who wrote a coffee-table book called *Sex* that was so steamy it was shipped to stores individually shrink-wrapped.

But motherhood changes everything, don't it, Madge?

We're always reading about what a strict mom Madonna has turned out to be. If young Lourdes doesn't pick up her clothes off the floor, they're thrown out "to teach her a lesson."

She's not allowed to watch TV ("rots the mind") or eat any junk food ("rots the body.") And Madonna famously wouldn't let the kid try out for a movie role because she wanted her to have as normal a childhood as possible. As though any kid whose nappies were designed by Versace could have a normal childhood.

Madonna admits to being furious when her ten-year-old wears jeans that are too tight.

So far, it seems as if Lourdes' childhood is shaping up to be almost as much fun as toe fungus.

Who would've imagined it? Madonna's conservative views on child-rearing make Laura Bush look like a hillbilly heroin-addicted pole dancer by comparison.

She has even announced that she wants Lourdes to wear her Stella McCartney–designed wedding gown when she walks down the aisle, like a virgin of course.

The gown is, I'm sure, sitting in a box somewhere having been dutifully "preserved" at the dry-cleaners just like any good Southern mama would do.

Madonna appears to be channeling the hopes and dreams of the Birmingham, Alabama, Junior League mom rather than the cone-bra wearing slut puppy we thought we knew.

Naturally, I agree with Madonna on all this stuff. We've told our kid that she won't be allowed to date until she's about thirty-two and then only with her daddy and me riding in the backseat. Sure, the sound of our his-and-her oxygen tanks clicking away will be somewhat disruptive but so be it.

If you think Madonna and I are overreacting consider that just last week one of the little boys in my kid's fourth grade class called her a "h-o-e ho!" Clearly he didn't mean that she was a garden tool. And clearly, my Precious is no ho or hoe. Dude just knew it was a bad word for girls.

The same day, I saw an article in *Seventeen* magazine that showed, with graphic illustrations, how to help your boyfriend put on a condom.

Because only a loser seventeen-year-old would actually read *Seventeen*, it's not lost on me or Madonna that this stuff is being read by girls more in the thirteen to sixteen range.

Although never by our girls of course.

The thing that Madonna will never have to contend with that every Southern mother trying to raise a decent daughter must deal with is the damn beauty pageant.

Look, y'all, for the last time, pageants are moneymakers. They don't give a shit about your kid. Didn't any of y'all see *Little Miss Sunshine*?

As Sophie retrieved the mail not long ago, I cringed when I saw the return address: The National American Miss Junior Pre-Teen Pageant.

"Throw that crap away," I told her.

"You shouldn't say 'crap'," she said.

"You're right, honey. Throw that shit away."

"But it says right here that I could be America's next National American Miss Junior Pre-Teen!"

"Pageants are for morons, kitten," I said.

"Jennybeth is in pageants all the time," Soph said, citing the one kid in her class that I absolutely can't stand. I know you should love all children, even the homely ones, but I just can't. I'll leave that to Brad and Angelina 'cause, shit, they can always buy the kid a new face or, in Jennybeth's pageant-obsessed case, personality.

"This one says it's different," said Soph. "Just look at the literature."

A few minutes later, I realized that perhaps I'd judged this pageant too harshly.

Turns out that this would be the one and only kid pageant that was about putting kids first! I know it's true because they said so!

"Your little girl will make new friends and have a fabulous time—we're waiting for *her*!"

OK, that's about a ten on the Creep-o-meter. I'll just bet you're waiting for her.

All we'd need was $380 in sponsorship money before my daughter would "reach her potential" and find out "how far her dreams can take her!"

They were very careful to avoid any mention of actually having a beauty requirement, but they did manage to discreetly request a "recent photo." I suppose this is just in case you have, like, a baby's arm growing out of the top of your head or something.

I apologize! That was cynical! Shame on me! I have to say

the pageant had thought of everything. They even promised to send us tips on how to find sponsors. A less worldly person might consider this a rip-off or even exploitation but, people, pageants are massively big, expensive productions that require, according to the literature, *florists!*

And you don't want some cheesy sound and lighting system, do you? Heaven's no! Not at the fabulous Renaissance Suites Hotel, which just happens to be Official Pageant Headquarters and has in-room movies and ice machines on odd-numbered floors that makes it just about as close to heaven as any of us can ever hope to get, am I right?

Of course, the pageant would require you to model a fancy dress, which might set you back a few hundred bucks, but it's worth it! Poise, presentation, and personality (the 3 Ps!) count for thirty percent each with ten percent for "community involvement," which turned out to be donating a book or stuffed animal to a good cause. Whew. That was easy. What if we had honestly had to get involved in our community? Ick.

Still the notion of securing sponsors for Sophie's entry sounded daunting at first. But then I read further and the pageant had helpful hints for how to approach prospective sponsors such as our dentist, hairdresser, or the owners of favorite local restaurants. Imagine how glad they'll be to see us!

And here was the best part: If Sophie didn't win the poise and presentation, she could still win in the "optionals" category, which is probably where they'd send the girl with the baby arm in her head right away. You could actually win a six-foot-tall trophy for selling the most advertising for the program!

Sure, it doesn't sound all that glamorous, but a girl has to start somewhere, right?

12

Britney's To-Do List: Pick Okra, Cover That Thang Up

❧

An Open Letter to Britney Spears 'cause she needs to hear it, y'all. . . .

Dear Brit:

Girl, I know you don't know me but you have to trust me on this: I have your back. For real.

Through all the wild partying and head-shaving and fornicating and tattooing and what not, I've got your back. Even though, when you shaved your head, you looked like the world's only redneck Tibetan monk. ("Y'all, let's chant and make some more of them sand pixtures, OK, y'all?") I didn't lose faith in you.

Why am I still loyal to you despite everything? Simple. You are me, only with money. OK, and youth and talent and a fairly serious substance abuse problem, but none of that matters, girl, 'cause you are a Southerner and a mama and that makes us sisteren.

Brit, you're just a good redneck girl who has, by determination, looks, and savvy management, propelled you and your little family out of Bigfoot, Louisiana, and into Malibu.

When I think about your rise to stardom, I hear the bouncy lyrics to The Beverly Hillbillies *playing in my head. "Kinfolks said, Brit move away from here; Californy is the place you oughta be, so they loaded up the truck and they moved to Bev-er-ly. . . ."*

But Brit, you're a Southern mama and, although you tried your best to fit in with the high-colonic-addicted Skeletors, at the heart of it, you can't escape the truth that you're just a good ol' Luzianna girl who knows what it's like to get your hands all scratched up picking okra out of Paw-Paw's garden.

Brit, a friend from your hometown e-mailed me not long ago and said she knew you'd gone ape-shit crazy because you didn't go home for Mardi Gras or Fat Tuesday or none of it. Girl, you can't get above your raisin' like that. Your precious babies need you to show them what the world outside of Hollywood is like.

When you didn't go home to the bayou, it spoke volumes. Didn't your mama have a pot of gumbo simmering on the back of that Kenmore Elite you bought her? I bet she did.

You should've been bouncing those baby boys on your legs and feedin' 'em spoon bread dripping in butter, not cavorting all over Nastytown showing your bidness to strangers.

But, I repeat, I have your back. It may not sound like it but I do. When you were pregnant with either Sean Preston or Jayden, I forget which, I remember thinking, now that's a girl who hasn't forgotten how Southern women eat when they're pregnant.

Unlike the other Hollywood mommies, who were living off sea urchin flakes and the like, you were eating real food: meat loaf, creamed potatoes, squash casserole. Good baby-growing food!

Britney, you kept it real out in L.A., even bravely denouncing that brief flirtation with Kabbalah you had on account of they were always hassling you for money and you were like, "Dude, I get enough of that from my baby-daddy."

OK, what you really said was that you kicked the centuries old Jewish mysticism to the curb because "Sean Preston is my religion, now, y'all."

I heard that.

Girl, when all the haters were saying you shouldn't be riding around with Sean P. in your lap like your very own personal little corn-rowed airbag, I still had your back.

Look, I remember what it was like to have a four-month-old in the house. You get so tired that you commit all kinds of dumb acts. How else can I explain all those Marie Osmond porcelain dolls ordered off QVC that now sit in my hall closet collecting dust?

Brit, I have no actual memory of ordering those dolls because I was so damn sleep deprived when my baby was little that there's no telling what I did. So riding around with a kid strapped to your boobs while driving isn't a huge shock to me.

Look, even when Sean Preston had to go to the hospital for a bruised noggin after falling out of his high chair, I didn't blame you; I blamed your mo-ron nanny. That chick must have been Tori Spelling stupid to blow a pie job like working for you. Listen, girl. If you'd let me baby-sit those boys I promise I'd never take my eyes off of either one of them. I mean never. *Think Rosie O' Donnell looking at an éclair or Charlize Theron.*

That's what I'm talking about.

OK, and when you nearly dropped Sean P. while walking down the steps at The Plaza, everybody was hating on you again and I'm like, "Hell-o, y'all, she was walking and holding a baby and chewing gum all at the same time and, well, that's a lot of multitasking."

And, Brit, just when things were really looking bad, they showed you driving around town with Sean P. facing forward in his little car seat.

Girl, in the South, we don't really pay attention to forward or backward all that much, but you're in Hollywood now.

Always remember that the kid has to face the rear *of the car because that way if y'all get hit from behind, the kid can be more helpful in providing information for the inevitable deposition. Hollywood types love to sue one another. They are very litigious. It's a big word; look it up. Get smart for your babies!*

Brit, the problem, as I see it, is that you had two babies in twelve months. This has caused you go astronaut-lady-in-diapers levels of crazy and nobody seems to understand that.

Nobody except me. I feel ya. Even Tom Cruise, the King of Crazy, would have to examine the evidence and conclude that you've gone and gotten yourself a bad case of postpartum depression. Hell, it's as plain as the new nose on Cameron Diaz's face.

I have to admit I expected more criticism from Tom, but I guess he was too busy to take a break from his creepy obsessive fetal sonogramming of his own kid to worry 'bout you. Still I thought sure that he'd saddle up his high horse and demand that you and every woman who ever had PPD be stoned in the town square or what passes for one in Beverly Hills, Barneys. And by stoned, I don't mean "high" like you were when you checked into Promises for the eleventy billionth time, bless your heart.

Why can't people see that so many of your problems are caused by having to live your life in front of those hideous paparazzi, who, incidentally, murdered our Princess Diana?

When you didn't strap your babies into their car seats correctly, it was, as you said, because you were "instinctively taking measures to protect your children" by quickly fleeing the photographers.

Brit, I like that you invoked a mother's instincts. I'll buy it. Only the snarkiest person would sneer at this and go, "Yeah, just as pioneer woman and cave woman before her took measures to flee the rabid paparazzi roaming the shops and eateries of Rodeo Drive."

Instinct is real, y'all. Perhaps it does kick in the same primal response and adrenaline rush that allows petite soccer moms to lift Suburbans with their bare hands to free trapped toddlers.

Or maybe not.

Either way, Brit, I still have your back. Gawd, it's not like you dangled your kids from a balcony like Michael Jackson. Who, by the way, I still get mad at when I think about that fool going to court every day with his personal magician. I don't even have a regular dry cleaner and he's got a personal magician? Asshole.

But, Brit, girl, as much as I love you, I will confess that there have been times where I just felt like I was duty-bound to jump on a jet, economy-class of course, and deal with you myself.

When I read that your mama and your daddy and your sister weren't able to talk sense into you, I practically wept.

Brit, you've got to just pick yourself up from this bad publicity, put on your big-girl panties (oh, hell, any panties at all at this point), and start taking care of yourself and your boys.

Postpartum or not, Southern mamas don't act like you're acting, hanging around those toxic twits Paris Hilton and Lindsay Lohan and the like.

Seriously, girl, it's not like you busted up with George Clooney, which would explain a lot of acting out and bad behavior. This was K-Fed. You should be over him in less time than it would take to microwave a bowl of grits.

Take a cue from another Southern mama who is going through a bumpy detour on love's highway, Reese Witherspoon. Reese is divorcing the father of her precious children whose name I forget, but sounds like he's French so who the hell cares about him anyway. Even so, with all her troubles, you don't see Reese Witherspoon putting skanks on speed dial as a coping mechanism.

Brit, you gotta stop flashing your lady parts for every creep with a camera phone or you're going to lose custody for good and your kids will end up playing with their Tonka trucks in the dirt yard of K-Fed's newest baby-mama's doublewide.

Trust me; I'm, like, psychic on this shit.

Listen, I know that K-Fed would probably make an OK daddy, but Southern women don't give up their young'uns no matter what.

Your babies are beautiful, but, let's face it, there's a lot of competition out there in Hollywood and you need to be a stand-up mama or they'll get lost in the celebrity shuffle.

With the birth of Suri Cruise and Brad and Angelina's Shiloh, there's going to be a lot of competition for the really good slots in day care, girl. You gotta clean up your act. You know it's going to be hard to be a kid in the same class with Shiloh. When you're the first member of the new super race, there's bound to be pressure.

Poor Suri Cruise will have to go to school with a bag on her head in comparison.

Still, most Hollywood types are crazy so you may be OK if you don't do anything else nutty.

Where, sistah-girl, was the outcry when Tom Cruise told everybody that he wanted to eat his baby's placenta and umbilical cord when she was born?

Later, he tried to say he was just kidding around but I think that was only because the press caught on that every time he said it, Katie Holmes was seen sticking her formerly Catholic finger down her throat and going, "Ewwww, nasty!"

Brit, she's just a regular girl like you, at heart. You can take the girl out of a dingy Ohio town, force her to have a Scientology-style "silent birth," and even make her have six inches sawed off her ankles so she'll be shorter than you, but she's still going to believe certain things are gross.

To be fair, eating stuff like that isn't all that weird except in America. Face it. We're a pretty provincial bunch. But the truth is that millions of people dine on placentas and umbilical cords every day in this world. Sure, they think it's the McDonald's Filet-O-Fish sandwich, but still.

To borrow a word from "W," Tom gets to be the decider on this sort of personal matter.

And it is terribly mean of us to suggest that Suri was some sort of Scientology experiment, that emerged from Holmes' rent-a-womb clothed in flowing white robes and reading a script for her first mindless sitcom.

Brit, you know how cruel Hollywood can be, don't you? So it was probably no surprise to you that when little Suri Cruise was only a few days old, people forgot about her and thought only of the long-awaited spawn of the Pitt/Jolie Nation. I refer again to baby Shiloh Pitt, lovingly called "just a blob" by Angelina, who had fervently hoped that, somehow, she would be able to physically give birth to a severely malnourished five-year-old African orphan instead of a stunning, plump blond American baby whose perfect bright eyes and smile merely mock everything her mother stands for.

Meanwhile, Brad has been completely emasculated, unlike your Kevin. How many times have we seen photos of Brad and Angelina walking down the beach? Well, Angelina's walking, with the Pacific breezes fluffing her perfect mane like a Pantene commercial, while former hunk Brad chugs dutifully behind, toting children, his fisherman's-knit sweater covered in snot. She is proud and strident. He is, well, Gilligan.

Whither People *magazine's Sexiest Man Alive?*

Truth is, Brad is so eager to please his woman that he's become

Hollywood's cutest drone, a hunky package of buzz kill who will no longer talk about his career "when, like, billions of people are starving to death."

This is certainly admirable to a point, but it's gotten to the place where Matt Lauer can't even offer Brad a cup of coffee without being subjected to a PowerPoint on the low wages of non-fair-trade bean growers.

(At about the same time, Jennifer Aniston and Vince Vaughn were cracking themselves up making pooty noises with their armpits.)

Brad wants everyone to know that he is more than a pretty face. Yes, we see that. Angelina, with her mysterious and mighty powers, has somehow given him a big ol' brain. Still, I suspect he's riding for a fall. Angelina is not of this world. As she flies her own plane around the world, rescuing the downtrodden and sick, she is more like a really hot Mother Teresa. How could one man keep up?

Brit, Brad is going to fall into that dark hole where all men go when they're with women who are more famous or powerful than them. Should they marry (a mistake), will Brad become like Dolly Parton's husband? Someone you think is still alive but you're never quite sure?

Brit, all this is by way of saying that I think the best hope you have to deflect all the awful criticism of your behavior is to point out that there are plenty of parents who are crazier than you. Create a distraction. Every time somebody photographs you with three cigarettes dangling out of your mouth at the same time, just say, "At least I didn't want to eat my baby's placenta, y'all." Or "At least I never called my kid a blob."

Brit, it's OK if you don't always feel like a natural mama. These *things take time and you're having to do it all in front of the whole wide world.*

Truth is, I'm not that great at it. People often insist on showing me pictures of their babies until I dutifully recite, "Oh, isn't she precious?" If this seems, somehow, insufficient, I'll manage something like, "Oh, I could just eat her up!"

The truth is, all babies look basically alike, except for Shiloh Pitt who, this just in, has won "America's Top Model 2020."

Brit, here's the way I see it. If you lay low, get sober, and tend to business on the home front, you can put all this unpleasantness behind you.

It won't be easy, girl, but you can do it. Just remember who you are and return to your Southern soul. Go home to the bayou; pick some okra and sing in the church choir.

It'll fix what ails you.

Love,

Mama Celia

13

(School) Uniformly Opposed to Everything

The Super Mommies were at it again at my kid's elementary school and they decided that nothing would do but that we start requiring the kids to wear uniforms.

Their reasons sounded noble enough: If everyone dresses alike, no one will pick on anyone because their clothes aren't as nice; if everyone dresses alike, students will concentrate on their studies, not on silly fluff like fashion; if everyone dresses alike, there's a chance you could take somebody else's better-behaved, smarter kid home with you and nobody would even notice for at least a couple of hours.

OK, I made the last one up, but I still didn't believe their arguments about why we needed to dress our kids in a mind-numbingly dull assortment of navy skorts, khaki pants, and white Polo shirts. And, let me revisit that first one: Skorts. This is like the creepy incestuous marriage of shorts and skirts. Get it? It's a skirt in the front and pants in the back and ugly all over. Think of it as fashion's cruel answer to designing one single garment as hideous as grown-up culottes for the grades K–5 set.

I didn't buy the argument that uniforms would improve grades because I did a little research and, turns out, that's not true at all according to loads of studies by people who have de-voted their lives to studying this important shit. The truth was, if you believed uniforms would improve grades, there was statisti-cally just as good a chance that you'd believe a tooth will dissolve overnight when placed in a glass of Coca-Cola or that a toddler in Texas died from rattlesnake bites after playing in the ball pit at Burger King. In other words, face it: You're a dumbass.

I sniffed a wharf rat from the beginning. And then it dawned on me: The real reason they wanted uniforms is that way your public school kid will look like he's going to private school and you'd look like a rich mommy as you hauled your matching children to the grocery store after school.

"Oh, my!" people would say in the checkout line. "They're sending three kids to private school. They must have lots of money. I want to be just like them."

"That's ridiculous," said Super Mommy Claire, when I posed my theory. "Only you would come up with such a negative motive."

Claire said that, truthfully, she didn't care about the cliques or the grades or any of that. It's just that uniforms would make her life easier.

"With uniforms, it's so easy and quick for them to get dressed in the morning," she said. "No more fights!"

"Great," I said. "If easy is the goal, why not just make them sleep in their clothes the night before? That'll really save some time."

Because we live in a democracy, despite the best efforts of Karl Rove, the parents were asked to vote either for or against uniforms and invited to speak out on why we were voting one way or the other.

I have to admit, I wasn't terribly articulate when it came time to debate the question, managing a less-than-compelling "Well, duh, they're ugly." It was a lightweight but passionate and strangely Valley Girl–sounding argument, but it was the best I could come up with on short notice.

I was hoping for more of an "Ask not what you can do for your country" kind of effect but, alas, the words didn't come and I sounded, well, whiny. I wanted to talk about the snuffing out of creativity and individuality and how this soul-sucking sameness will destroy their little spirits and turn talented teachers into the dress-code police for much of the day instead of allowing them to do what they do best—teach—but my mind went blank and I just said, "And in conclusion, like I said earlier, they're ugly. Thank you America and, well, all of our Allies and all the ships at sea."

The ballots were quickly counted and I wondered if my

dough-brained protest, which was only slightly more articulate than that of, say, Scooby-Doo, caused the parents to vote in favor of uniforms 2–1.

I should be used to being in the minority. Rarely do I vote for a president who wins, except for Gore and I believe we all know how well that turned out. So, for a time, I felt ostracized at my kid's school, *mama non grata*. I had become the poo in the punchbowl, the Mel Gibson at the bar mitzvah.

"You'll love these uniforms with time," said Claire, who was one of the handful of mommies that would still be seen talking to me. "They're practically indestructible. You could drop nuclear waste on these things and it would just bounce right off."

Hey, now that would make a great science fair project, I thought.

There was only one way I was going to ever fit in with the Popular Mommies and that would be to make sure that they understood that even though I hated the uniforms, I was still a team player, more or less.

The perfect science fair project would show that I was a truly committed parent, not just some negative naysayer who always showed up just a little bit drunk at PTA pizza night.

Oh, shut up. It's not like I didn't have a driver and how else is any human expected to make it through the obligatory thirty-minute treasurer's report, with its talk of fund balances and transfers and other things that I can't believe I'm hearing instead of being home watching *Deal or No Deal*.

With Precious wearing the odious skort at dinner that night, the three of us discussed her science fair entry.

"I was thinking," I started, feeling pretty confident, "what if we went to the mall and dropped a five-dollar bill on the floor and then saw how many people would return it to us and how many would just keep it."

There. That was *awesome*. I waited for hubby and Precious to applaud.

And waited some more.

Hubby: "That's the dumbest idea I ever heard. That's not science. It's human behavior. Don't you know the difference?"

Me: (Silent)

Hubby: "OK, how about this?" (His eyes were doing that shifty thing they do when he either has a great idea or has just farted in public. Which, I might add, is never a great idea.)

Me: (Silent *and* pissed)

Hubby: "Well, don't you want to hear it?"

Precious: "I don't think Mommy's talking to you anymore. Go ahead and tell me."

"I was just thinking that we could replicate an experiment that I read about in which you can actually change the molecular structure of a water crystal by exposing it to words, pictures, and even soothing music. Then all we'd have to do is photograph it with a special macro lens and using the research facilities of a major university we could develop some amazing slides that illustrate the aesthetics and the quantity of the crystals."

Our jaws dropped.

Finally, I spoke.

"You're going to talk to water? Nobody's going to believe an eight-year-old came up with that. Hey! I've got an idea. What if we all eat a bunch of beets and then write about how it makes your pee turn purple?"

"Oh, great," hubby sneered. "Why don't we make a baking soda volcano? Now that's something nobody has *ever* thought of doing."

"Tornado in a bottle?" I offered brightly.

"Arrrrgggh."

"There's no need to get snippy," I said. "How about this? What if we spread a dirty rumor about somebody and then sit back and see how long it takes to get back to us?"

"That's not science!" he shrieked. "That's Telephone."

His eyes were seriously dancing in his head now. I was afraid he was going to go all *A Beautiful Mind* on us and start writing shit on the walls.

"Well, have you got any more ideas, Mr. Wizard?"

"Yes, as a matter of fact I do," he said. "We could change carbon into iron or even build a homopolar generator."

I snickered. "Not that there's anything wrong with that."

"I said homo*polar*," hubby snapped. "What are you? Two? Look, I have another idea. We could build an interferometer. It's sort of a squealing wall."

"I think they've got some of those at Chuck E. Cheese's," I said. "Now if you'll excuse me, I'm going to go talk to some Chardonnay and see if it has anything to say back."

14

Slacker Moms Don't Have
a Ghost of a Chance

⌇

The annual science fair came and went and the Princess actually made it to "alternate," which meant that she was almost, but not quite, good enough to go to the next level of competition. As it turned out, we had settled on a fabulous experiment called "Is Daddy Making Us Sick?" which used petri dishes to determine that, yes, if Daddy drinks milk from the carton, there is a transfer of his mouth germs to the liquid and so we're all basically just lucky to be alive.

The judges praised her science project and, with the new "alternate" status, I sensed it wouldn't be long before I was back in the good graces of the Popular Mommies, including some who were still smarting a bit from my anti-uniform rant.

You're probably wondering why I care so much about the Popular Mommies' opinion of me and I will not lie to you.

See, if you aren't in good with the mommies of your kid's friends, you can't in good conscience call on them to help you with after school child care when you really need it. Or, as Hillary Rodham Clinton says, "It takes a village, assholes."

For instance, if you can only get a mani/pedi or hair color appointment at three in the afternoon, it doesn't take long to realize that the whole picking-up-the-kid-at-school thing is going to screw that up.

Oh. You thought I meant that I needed child care help so I could volunteer with the local bloodmobile or some such?

Are you high? Y'all know me better'n that by now.

Of course, I'm not above lying to make it *sound* more noble. After all, the mommies might not appreciate the truth, that I had TiVo'd every episode of *Friday Night Lights* and really needed some alone time to watch each episode.

You can't ask somebody to baby-sit your kid for free just so you can catch up on your must-see TV. That's nuts. So you tell them something more palatable where everybody's a winner. Something like: "Can you please take Precious home with you after school today? I have to donate an organ to a needy person, but I should be done with that by, oh, say six o'clock. It's just a spleen or somethin'."

Of course, on another level, it gnawed at me a bit that my baby's science project was only an "alternate."

It was like being the first runner-up in a beauty pageant or lieutenant governor or even vice president. These are positions that are historically lackluster. Why do you think Cheney shot that old man in the face? Every now and then you want it to be all about *you*.

"What does 'alternate' mean?" Soph asked that night.

"It means that if something happens to one of the six *real* winners, you get to take their place and advance in the competition."

"You mean like if they got sick or something?"

"Yes, or if someone planted a rumor that they bought the whole project on the Internet and had it overnighted from some smart kid in Wisconsin."

"Mommy, you didn't!"

No, I didn't. But it was tempting. Sometimes it's exhausting trying to stay in good with the Popular Mommies, even if it is just for selfish reasons. They're always coming up with new ways to stress me out.

Standing outside our cars in the pickup line at carpool one afternoon, I overheard them comparing their teacher gifts, to be presented on the last day of school.

Teacher gifts?

I don't remember that one when I was growing up. If we gave our overworked, underpaid teachers anything at all, it was probably an awkward hug and a promise to (snicker, snicker) "read a lot over the summer."

But the teacher gift is a Requirement now. It's like the horrifically named "pushing gift" that is now presented from husband to wife practically at the moment the bundle of joy is being propelled into a world in which there are more votes for *American Idol* contestants than the U.S. president (sad) but offers 182 choices of presweetened breakfast cereal (happy). I have known women who clamped their thighs shut and refused to deliver their baby until their own duh-hubby had shown up with sufficient bling.

Doctor: "Push, Mrs. Lardbottom! Push! It's tiiiiiimmme!"

Mrs. L.: "Right away, doctor. Just a minute. Darius, where's my pushing present? This is when you're supposed to give it to me. Darius?"

Darius: "Huh? Pushing present? What's that?"

Doctor: "I can see the head now. This baby is coming! Push now. One . . . two . . ."

Mrs. L.: "Oh, this baby ain't coming into a world where his cheap bastard daddy didn't even have sense enough to buy me a pushing present. Forget that shit."

Doctor (getting impatient): "Look, Mr. Lardbottom, just give her the present. (then, cheerily) This little one is ready to meet his parents!"

Darius Lardbottom: "But, but, er, I don't have anything."

Doctor: (removing gloves, paper gown, and hat) "Then I believe that my work here is done."

The Perfect, Popular Mommies look down their surgically altered noses at the loser mommies who don't buy anything for the teacher at the end of the year or, worse, give Avon.

It's yet another area in which they get to do the Mommy

Superior dance. They know that it's equally crucial to get the teacher gift in on time and with a MVA (maximum viewing audience).

See, if you get the teacher gift in too late, no one will know all the time and effort and expense you went to. Except the teacher, which, I realize, should be the point, but that doesn't get you anywhere when it comes to impressing the Other Mommies.

This fierce, and completely unnecessary, desire to be the best mommy is bigger than us. Why do you think so many of us are turning to meth?

No, sorry. What I meant to say was, why do you think so many turn to professional party planners and life coaches and therapists and Ben & Jerry's Chunky Monkey eaten by the pint in the blue glow of infomercials for thirty-dollar spaghetti drainers hours after everyone else has gone to bed? Not me, mind you, but others I've heard about. . . .

Some of these Perfect Mommies are responsible for a ghastly new trend that is sweeping the country.

Called "ghosting" for Halloween or "elving" for Christmas, I am "barfing" at the notion that, at the end of a day of work, laundry, carpooling, cooking, and helping with homework, all I want to do is look at my front door and discover a white ghost-shaped cutout attached to a bag of treats. There are instructions attached, telling me that I must now skulk around in the dark and place my own homemade treats in bags for two new victims, er, neighbors?

I'm not thinking this is what the dead kid meant in the movie when he advised everybody to "pay it forward."

A friend who has exhaustedly been "ghosted" at home and even at work, says she's just churning the stuff.

Brilliant!

She and I think it's possible that only one sucker actually baked treats a few weeks ago and the rest of us are just passing them along until they get really moldy.

It didn't take me long to figure out a way around this foolishness. You simply tack a ghost cutout you've made yourself on your door and they'll think you've already been ghosted. It's just like Passover in the Bible, only without the mess and fuss of putting blood on your door.

I believe my idea is worthy of a Nobel Prize or at least a "No Doorbell" prize.

To the mommies who came up with this nonsense for the holidays, let me just say that you just need to go out and get yourself a good old-fashioned, feet-to-Jesus orgasm and you need to do it yesterday.

You are obviously under a *lot* of stress.

Like teacher gifts and all the rest of it, this is the sort of stuff that only a woman would inflict on another woman.

Can you in your wildest dreams see a bunch of men sitting around talking about ways to share treats with neighbors, making it fun for the kids and lots of work for them?

You can? Oh, sorry. I meant *straight* men.

Men get a lot of things wrong, but one thing they all excel

in is their absolute total commitment to never adding a bunch of useless crap to their day just because "it sounds cute!"

You think a man is going to sit up all night cutting out little white paper ghosts or green and red elves to attach to a bag of homemade candies?

Oh, hail no. Not as long as we live in America and there's still porn on the Internet.

You think a man is going to put up with tying little multi-colored yarns to the bag and handwriting the "ghosting instructions"? See above.

These very specific rules require that the treats be left in a brown lunch sack on the doorstep, accompanied by The Official Ghosting (or elving, or leprechauning, or Easter bunnying, etc.) poem which you've hand copied just for them.

The last time somebody left something on my doorstep in a brown paper sack, it wasn't candy and it damn sure wasn't edible. It was also on fire, but that's another story.

And don't we already have enough crap to do during the holidays? Elving adds just one more level of horror to a Christmas to-do list that's already as bloated as Kim Jong Il after his weekly pork rind binge.

Of course, I have been criticized for not being enthusiastic about this "neighborhood bonding exercise."

Hey, I didn't choose my neighbors. I don't want to get to know them better. I just want to take a stroll at night, dart about the hedges beneath their windows, flatten my body to the ground and wait until it's safe to look through their open drapes to see if any of them have anything that I'm jealous of. Is that so crazy?

Besides, you know how neighborhoods change all the time. You never know who's moving in or who's been kicked out.

I'll miss ol' Darius Lardbottom.

15

Nature Deficit Disorder Is Naturally Upsetting

❧

Like a lot of kids her age, my Princess is big into music, mostly pop and rock listened via sparkly ear buds hooked into her MP3 player. It's a constant companion, this little gizmo that can hold hundreds of songs so that you are guaranteed that you will never have to experience the horror of a quiet, utterly still and silent moment no matter where you are.

She likes Gavin DeGraw, Hellogoodbye, Fall Out Boy, Panic! at the Disco, and a bunch of other people I'm too uncool to recognize.

Sometimes I can barely suppress an urge to tell her about the truly great rock and roll bands. I want to put on a cardigan (because frankly it's cold all the time lately) and tell her that back in my day, you had "your Led Zeppelin, your King Crimson, your Jethro Tull" and so forth. I don't think she'd care much, though.

Soph and her little friends walk around with their iPods and MP3s hooked to them like tiny rhinestone-dotted colostomy bags. They wouldn't think of leaving home without their tunes.

Which is why I've decided that one way to make the Princess listen to me would be to reach her through music, a medium that she obviously is passionate about.

Moms all over this great land have their own *Greatest Hits* or *Best of* collections with them at all times, these mantras that we repeat all day, eighty times a day, to our kids. Sadly, our nagging "hits" aren't nearly as much fun as Fergie describing why she's so *Fergalicious* or Nelly Furtado boasting of being a *Promiscuous Girl.* Double ick.

It almost makes me nostalgic for those dreadful Kidz Bop CDs favored by the five-year-old set and featuring the annoyingly wholesome vocal stylings of a fresh-faced bunch of kidz who just want to grow up and marry their own Usher some day, even the boys.

You won't find my "greatest hits" on the shelves at Best Buy or even the scruffy-but-cool independent store where the sales guy has a barbell in his tongue and keeps trying to sell me Rage Against the Machine, and I'm thinking how does this weird barbell guy know about my ongoing problem with my overpriced piece-of-crap vacuum cleaner?

Mom's Greatest Hits won't make it to the Billboard charts

but it might sell well on one of those late-night TV commer-cials if I can scrape together enough dough for the studio time to actually lay down some tracks. (That's music lingo to you ordinary cats; try to hang.)

Unlike other mail-order CDs such as *Music From the Godfa-ther,* as played on the pan flute, my greatest hits are targeted to moms like me. Here's a sampling from my unofficial, yet-to-be-rcleased CD:

Make Up Your Bed, Make Up Your Bed, Makc Up Your Bed, Make Up Your Bed (Oh, and one other thing: Make Up Your Bed).

And who can forget the classic stylings of:

Don't Talk to Strangers (I Don't Wanna See Your Puppies, Perv, But Hey My Mom Loved Thriller*).*

The hits just keep coming with:

Eat Your Vegetables, Eat Your Vegetables, Eat Your Vegeta-bles, Eat Your Vegetables (Oh, and One Other Thing: Make Up Your Bed).

And who can resist the classic chart-topper:

No, Hell, No, You Can't Have a Guinea Pig (Until You Can Prove You're Responsible Enough to Take Care of It).

Admittedly, it's hard to compete with the music kids really like so you'd have to have cool artists record *Mom's Greatest Hits.*

Beyoncé could be pointing to the laundry basket that needs to go downstairs when she's saying "to the left, to the left" instead of a cheating lover being instructed on how to get out of her house pronto.

As in:

You Must Not Know 'Bout Me (I'm the One That Won't Let You Go to the Sleepover 'Til You've Cleaned Your Room).

When they're not listening to music, kids are playing video or computer games.

And when I tell my kid that she and her friends should play outside, they just stare at me like I'm Psycho Environmentalist Chick.

I just think it's sad these kids don't know the sublime pleasure of trapping lightning bugs in a mayonnaise jar on a sultry summer evening, as I did as a child. I'll never forget the magic of watching these graceful, charming creatures glow orange and yellow, elegant little flashlights in the night darting about inside the jar until they finally collapsed into a dead, crunchy heap because, my bad, I'd forgotten the damn holes in the lid. Again.

At least I know I'm not alone in thinking that kids need to get outside and play.

A new study has found that children today have "Nature Deficit Disorder."

They've lost connection with nature, this generation that is nauseatingly fluent in Wii, MySpace, and *High School Musical.* When tested, only a few could identify a wild salamander or recognize poison oak.

To be honest, I don't know a wild salamander from a tame one, but I'm guessing that the wild ones party with Timbaland. I wondered how the Princess would do with a test on nature.

"In which direction does lichen grow on trees?" I asked her.

"I'm not sure," she said. "What's lichen, anyway?"

"I think I left a pot on the stove," I said.

Hey, the acorn didn't fall far from the lichen covered tree, now did it?

I've never been a big fan of the outdoors, particularly the part that's outside.

I've always been mildly suspicious of fresh air and exercise. People who camp always crow about how "food always tastes better outdoors!" No it doesn't. It tastes better indoors served on lovely china with napkins folded to resemble the backs of swans.

And although I know I should exercise more, I can't help thinking about that poor Chinese housewife who went for a hike and ended up having a two-inch-long leech stuck in her nose.

Turns out she paused on her long hike to splash some fresh water from a stream into her face. A tiny leech swam right up her left nostril.

Later, she would tell reporters that she wasn't worried about leeches in the water, explaining, "I'm used to seeing all these worms in the water while hiking."

OK, I have to throw up.

Anyway, two weeks later, she felt something strange in her nose. She went to the doctor who discovered the leech was getting bigger by the day.

At this point, I would've keeled over dead but this woman was tough, hons. The kind of woman who washes her face with worms. Doctors tried to remove it but were unsuccessful so it kept growing for another couple of weeks. If this leech had gotten any bigger, Angelina Jolie would've tried to adopt the sucka.

Finally, doctors sprayed the leech with a nasal spray chock full of anesthesia. After the Longest Two Minutes of Anyone's Life Ever, the leech slowly backed out of the woman's nostril and was gunned down by the S.W.A.T. team. OK, retrieved with forceps but you get it.

At this point, the woman ran screaming from the room and jumped out of a tenth-floor window, plummeting to her death. No, no really, she's fine.

All of which is by way of saying that hiking's bad and napkins shaped like swans are good.

So perhaps I'm partly responsible for my daughter's abysmal lack of knowledge about flora and, uh, the other one. Could she be suffering from Nature Deficit Disorder? And, if so, what was the cure?

That's easy. To combat this disorder, which, I'm guessing, is

easily diagnosed by detecting a fixed stare and excessive Chee-
tos orange dust around the mouth and fingertips, children suffering from NDD are being told to "climb trees, build forts,
and explore creeks."

And in possibly the weirdest marketing tie-in of all time,
even McDonald's and Hummer are helping find a cure.

My kid's Mega Happy Meal last week came packaged in
what looked to the jaded grown-up as an advertisement for a
Hummer. But no! Look closer! It's actually a moment in envi-
ronmental exploration brought to you by Hummer.

Is it just me or does anyone else find this as hilarious as the
phrase "Singer Paris Hilton"?

I read the Hummer Happy Meal "fun maze" copy with a
mixture of revulsion and admiration. You gotta have some
set of balls to suggest that you park your Hummer to "stop
for a hike" because "it's a fun way to see the outdoors and get
exercise!"

Yes, drive your eight-million-pound Barbie war machine
twenty miles so you can get some exercise. Makes perfect sense
to me!

At the end of a fun day of Hummer-inspired swimming,
hiking, and climbing you can "sleep under the stars."

Stars? What stars? Wasn't that the ozone you just burned
up?

My favorite suggestion was that the Hummer will help you
cross over a fallen tree on your path. Go ahead and run over
Susan Sarandon clinging to it while you're at it.

How fortunate that Hummer is here to help our nation with this awful epidemic of Nature Deficit Disorder!

Sure, it's a little like asking Michael Richards to emcee the Essence Awards but no matter. It's for the children.

I told Soph that she needed to unplug herself from that glittered colostomy bag and get outside and get some fresh air, experience nature up close and personal and she—being a Princess and all—said that was a great idea.

"It is?" I said, hopefully. Maybe that *Mom's Greatest Hits* was really helping.

"Sure. We'll go to Ulta and get some peach-pulp pedicure lotion 'cause that's very nature-y."

That's not exactly what I had in mind, but I shouldn't have been surprised that this was her take on "nature."

USA Today did a big story on how ten-year-old girls, who are notoriously suffering from NDD, are going to the spa for massages and facials these days.

What does a ten-year-old need a massage for? Tough afternoon of sitting around playing Dream Life got your neck muscles sore? Shopper-shoulder from hauling around bags full of overpriced T-shirts from Aberzombie?

Puleez.

Maybe I'm just jealous. I was forty before I got my first manicure and it just seems more than a little unfair that a ten-year-old is working in a mani-pedi between homework and oboe lessons.

While a facial would've been a good idea for those of us who grew up as teenagers in the pre-Accutane era, it's hard to figure out why a ten-year-old (or even younger according to the article), really needs one.

At that age, isn't it still OK for the banana-berry facial to be less from a fifty-dollar treatment administered by someone named Ramone and more from the yummy remnants of a Baskin-Robbins smoothie?

It's not just little girls, of course. There's also something called the "mini-metrosexual phenomenon." This explains the astounding success of preteen boys' body sprays such as Tag and Axe.

Clearly, we've come a long way from the date-night dousing of Brut that I remember gagging on in high school.

Still, there's something creepy about a ten-year-old boy fretting about hair products when he should be analyzing box scores or putting his sister's bra in the freezer. I mean, what kind of freaks are we raising these days?

Nature Deficit Disorder freaks, that's what kind.

Of course it's fun to dress up, experiment with makeup, and play big-girl hair. I mean you'd have to be Cruella De Vil mean not to allow that once in a while. But the notion of regular spa appointments for little girls sits with me like a bad fish taco.

I'm not ready for Sophie to breathlessly inform me that Rumi has had a cancellation by another "client" whose "like, grandmother died or something" so now she can get her hot-stone massage after all.

It started out innocently, I'm sure. Just another way for moms to bond with their daughters. But it's gotten out of hand

and now we have an entire industry catering to seven-year-olds who tweeze.

To them I just take a page from Hummer's playbook and advise them: Go climb a tree or something. Bark is great for exfoliation.

16

Make Your Own Damn Pancakes

Although I'm still not paying for my kid to have a spa day, until she can have hers at Fantastic Sam's like a good redneck girl, the message apparently isn't sinking in.

When I asked the Princess what kind of birthday party she wanted this year, she didn't hesitate: "A sleepover with professional salon makeovers for everybody and facials and hairdos and manicures and pizza and we'll give everybody AeroBeds with their names monogrammed on them in fancy hot pink thread and we'll go to the waterslide and the bowling alley and maybe a movie afterward."

"Do what?"

"Well, you asked me what I wanted," she said, bottom lip

out to here. "I was thinking we could get an artist to come and give all of us henna tattoos for our arms and our ankles and maybe a really big one around our *necks*! And we could *pierce each other's ears*!"

OK, as long as she keeps things within reason.

As I tried to recover from this announcement, Soph scampered off to find paper for a list of party supplies.

"We can rent a popcorn machine and a Slushie machine and have a make-your-own-sundae bar and we can make s'mores!" she said consulting a list entitled "Party Fun."

"Won't all that junk food make everybody hurl?" I asked.

She gave me a look that clearly said I was a dumbass.

"Nobody *ever* gets sick at a sleepover. They're too much *fun*!"

"What about the kid who got the 104-degree fever at your last sleepover and thought she was Willy Wonka?"

"Oh, that was just that one time."

On the appointed day, nine little girls arrived with sleeping bags, inflatable beds and apparently eighteen pairs of pajamas and twenty-two singing Hello Kitty toothbrushes apiece.

We'd downsized the party considerably (Slip 'n' Slide, cookout, and a movie shown outdoors and projected onto a white bedsheet) after I told the Princess a lot of parents might not be thrilled to discover that their daughters were freshly tattooed and pierced the next morning.

"What about spray tans?" she asked. "That would be cool."

I had a momentary flashback to a horrific tanning-bed scene in *Final Destination 3* in which two teenage girls are trapped in overheated tanning beds and their skin starts dripping off their bones like queso dip.

"No!!!!"

At the party, hubby and I realized that nine-year-old girls have extremely short attention spans.

"When are we eating?"

"Can she open presents now?"

"Is my arm broken? It really hurts. My daddy's a lawyer and he said that the Slip 'n' Slide is just a tort waiting to happen. Did you know that? Did you?"

"I'm going to ask you for two hamburgers but I'm really just going to eat one small bite out of one and say it tastes "too hamburgery."

(Crying) "She said I liked a *boy!*"

At exactly 1 A.M., my official lights-out deadline, I reminded the girls they'd better go to sleep or I'd have to stay up with them and then I'd be too tired to make pancakes that look like Hannah Montana the next morning.

"Really? You can make pancakes that look like Hannah Montana?" my kid asked.

"Of course not, but my wine buzz gave out, like, five hours ago and I gotta get some sleep. They'll understand."

Besides, if pressed, I could always just glue a photo cut out of *Tiger Beat* to the pancakes because Hannah (really Miley Cyrus) is the modern-day equivalent of Partridge Family heartthrob Keith Cassidy for "most pictures in a preteen magazine ever." And, yes, it's beyond unsettling that I know that.

When everything was dark and I was finally threading my

way around and between ten sleeping bags to head upstairs to bed, I heard a small voice.

"I forgot my white-noise fan."

Pretend I didn't hear that and keep heading for the stairs.

"Sophie's mom! I can't sleep without my white-noise fan. Do you hear me? *I can't sleep without it!!!!*"

Crapcrapcrapcrapcrap.

"OK, honey," I said with as much cheer as anyone could muster at one o'clock in the morning. "We'll figure something out."

"Just call my mom and dad. They'll bring it over."

"But, sweetie, your mom and dad live ten miles from here. It's one o'clock in the mother—, I mean it's one o' clock in the morning! We don't want to wake them up at this hour, do we?"

"They won't mind," she said. "They love me."

"Trust me," I said, patting her hair gently and looking at her sweet face in the soft moonlight streaming through the living room windows. "I'm sure your parents don't love you *that* much. No one does!"

Her eyes got all wide and wet like one of those Precious Moments dolls. What? What'd I say?

"Sweetie, it's like this. The big hand is on the twelve and the little hand is on the one. *Get it?* I'm not calling anybody at one o'clock in the morning unless it's the cops because a stranger with a bloody ax has stumbled in here and threatened to open our skulls like a pile of ripe nectarines. Now night-night."

OK, bad idea. There were now ten exceedingly hysterical little girls sitting bolt upright in their Diva sleeping bags.

"Mommy's just kidding," said Sophie. "She gets really cranky when she's tired and she says crazy stuff."

"So there's nobody with an ax coming to get us?" the sweet, shy kid who hadn't said a word all day asked. I just knew that before the night was over she was going to pee on my new couch.

"Of course not, darling," I said. "I'm just having some fun. Gawd, haven't y'all ever told spooky stories at a sleepover?"

What was wrong with me? Now I'd never get to sleep. Don't children have any sense of humor? I thought the ax nectarine thing was pretty funny, but kids? You can't make 'em laugh unless you fart.

While I pondered this in an exhausted haze, the clock ticked closer to 2 A.M. Finally, mercifully, I looked over and realized the little girl who needed her white-noise fan was sound asleep. I wanted to wake her up and tell her "Ha! You don't need that fan. You were *asleep*!" but that would have been self-defeating, I guess. Still, it has always been very important to me for everyone to know when I'm right about something. Which is basically all the time.

While some might say that's an annoying character trait, I would just say that's just one more thing they're wrong about. Being right all the time is a burden, people. Feel my pain.

Finally, one by one, the little girls began to wear themselves out. By two-thirty it was all quiet and I crept upstairs, finally, to sleep.

And wake up again at 6 A.M. Yes, three and a half hours. That's how long they slept before crawling out of their pink cocoons and deciding it was time to *play Twister*!

I punched duh-hubby to inform him that the girls were awake but he just mumbled "OK" and resumed snoring.

OK? No, not OK! He'd been asleep since 11 P.M. Where was the fairness in this?

Still, I knew in my heart that little girls get freaked out at the sight of men in boxer shorts and "Dook Sucks" T-shirts stumbling around in the early hours.

The sleepover is primarily the responsibility of the mommy-host and that will never change.

While hubby snoozed with a big smile on his face, I went downstairs to make the damned pancakes.

"These don't look like Hannah Montana!" one little girl screeched.

"Of course they do. Now just be quiet and drink your mimosa," I said. "Have a few, as a matter of fact. By the sixth one, the pancakes will look like any damn body you want 'em to!"

"Aaaaahhhhhh!!! You said the 'D' word. Sophie's mommy said the 'D' word."

I silently reached into my robe pocket and tossed a dollar into the Swear Jar on the kitchen counter.

I'd installed the Swear Jar a year earlier to curb the urge to cuss by any member of the family but, as of this moment, I had been the only one who had actually put any money into the jar. We'd emptied it at least three times.

I've always had a problem with "potty mouth" but the most embarrassing moment had happened years ago on the job.

As the wedding editor for the newspaper, I was used to dealing with demanding nut jobs day after day but one, in particular, led me to unleash a few well-chosens as soon as she was out of range.

A Yankee man I worked with stared at me, mouth agape.

"You eat with that mouth?" he asked.

I was mortified. To be corrected on manners by a Yankee man was beyond humiliating.

But here I was, cussing in front of a kitchen full of nine-year-olds. What was wrong with me?

Sleep deprivation, that's what.

Hubby emerged in jeans and a clean shirt, freshly showered and feeling energized by his undisturbed ten hours of sleep.

"Yummy! Something smells great! What's for breakfast, honey?"

"We're having pancakes that look just like Hannah Montana," I said sweetly.

"Really?" he said, scowling slightly at the griddle. "They don't look much like Hannah Montana to me."

I considered slamming his head into the griddle and asking him if he'd like to think again now that he had a closer look, but that would've resulted in having to put more money in the "Violent Behavior" jar, my latest anger-management tool for occasional perimenopausal outbursts.

"Sophie's mommy said the 'D' word," one little girl snitched to hubby with obvious delight.

"You got off lucky, kid," he said, reaching for the orange juice.

Four hours later, all the mommies arrived to pick up their little girls, who were all leaving with little director's chairs with their names on them that we'd used for the outdoor movie. All in all, it had been a pretty great party.

"Is it true that they only got three and a half hours sleep?" asked one of the more high-maintenance moms.

"Yep."

"And that you used the 'D' word and gave them mimosas?"

"Guilty as charged. Except their mimosas didn't have champagne in them. Who do you think I am? Michael Jackson?"

"And that you told them a man with a bloody ax was going to come through the door and chop them up like nectarines?"

"Of course not. You know, you can't believe everything a kid tells you."

The "Lies" jar is getting pretty full, too.

17

Christmas at the "Urgent" Care

~

If you plan to travel with children during the holidays, there's about a one-zillion-percent chance that you'll spend at least some part of "the most wonderful time of the year" in the urgent-care outpost of some town you've never heard of.

I'd hoped to avoid this feverish truth by demanding that everyone in the family use hand sanitizer roughly eighteen to twenty times a day during the month of December. Sadly, it didn't work.

As we sat for hour after hour in the Doctor's Immediately Urgent Prime and Emergent Medicinal Care complex, I pondered the hollow nature of those words: "urgent" and "immediate." I also comforted myself with the image of the

Silkwood-style hot shower I would take the moment we got out of there. Gawd, who would've thought there would be so many sick people in this place?

A few snarkily mentioned that they'd had time to write their wills during the wait and one claimed to have asked the receptionist to be his witness.

I'd worked so hard not to be here with the Princess, who sat silent and beet-red, occasionally rousing long enough to mutter the word "brandy" over and over. In fact, she had awakened me the night before to simply say "Brandy" and I just thought she was having some weird dream about that skinny singer with the so-so pipes and snotty attitude. It's not like we have a house full of snifters and ascots for shit's sake.

Because I'm a superstitious sort, I wondered if I had brought this misfortune upon us by failing to send Christmas cards this year. Out of time and patience, I'd announced that when it came to the whole buying, stamping, mailing thing? Over it. Duh-hubby said he'd do the Christmas cards this year, which was funny since he, like every other man I know, hasn't mailed a Christmas, birthday, or any other greeting card since the "I do"s were spoken. Women do all that stuff, even when it's *his* relatives. We're brain-dead that way.

Not sending Christmas cards was deliciously liberating.

I know I should've felt guilty about it but I just couldn't. When I think of all the years that I have agonized over our family Christmas card photo, I feel silly. There's real tragedy in the world, people. Cate Blanchett is down to, like, eighty-five pounds, y'all. Now that's something to worry about.

The Princess squirmed in her seat while I filled out the required paperwork and continued to wonder if my selfishness had somehow jinxed our holiday.

I had to giggle when I realized that one of the many forms I was filling out asked if my daughter, *the fourth grader,* was married.

"Should I fill this out?" I asked the receptionist, from behind the turtleneck I had neurotically pulled up over my nose.

"Oh, no. You're special," she said. "The forms are for all the *other* people to fill out."

Oh, snap!

"Brandy" came a small voice from across the room.

I returned to the plastic seat that had been factory-molded to most comfortably accommodate a chipmunk's ass and dutifully filled out the forms detailing my daughter's imaginary marriage and work history.

Yep, I was in some sort of Purgatory, that much was clear. It was because, this year, I hadn't "kept Christmas" as Aunt Sudavee used to say. I mean, not even close. She used to chide me when I was jealous of another kid's toy on Christmas morning.

"Envy is a sin. Get a cup o' Jesus!" she'd say, which sounded like good advice but still left me without an Etch A Sketch.

I was paying for not keeping Christmas. It was true. This year, for the first time, I didn't bake a single cookie for other people, yet had happily received plenty of cookies, including those fabulous little butterscotch haystack things you make with chow mein noodles, plus a big tin of rum balls that I had to fight off my yard guy to keep.

It wasn't all my fault. A lot of friends and family members had said they were taking steps to de-stress Christmas so I was just going along with others.

My sister-in-law had suggested that we skip presents altogether and spend more "real time" together doing meaningful things like constructing a gingerbread house together, singing carols around the piano and, in general, acting as if we were all Dickensian orphans trapped in a world without Neiman's. Sis-in-law had read a book about "unplugging the Christmas machine" and it made not doing stuff you didn't want to do sound almost noble.

Out of respect for sis-in-law's wishes, I didn't buy her a present but I hoped that she, in turn, would respect my wishes. For an iPod Nano and some really expensive chocolate, not those trifling Hershey Krackel bars everybody got last year.

Had my greed brought this plague unto our household? Verily, I thought so. Guilt overwhelmed me and I lowered my turtleneck, which had caused more than a few mean stares.

One hour later, the doctor was ready for us. I don't want to say he was young, but I could've sworn he'd trick-or-treated at my door in a Power Rangers costume just a couple of months earlier.

He stuck two cotton swabs into my daughter's precious nostrils for a flu test.

"Why'd he do that?" she asked groggily, after the tiny doctor had left the room.

"I don't know, honey, but in some countries, I think it means you're engaged."

After another fifteen minutes or so, the itty-bitty doctor returned and announced that it wasn't flu but "just, uh, some kind of, like, virus or somethin'."

"Righteous," I said. We left with a prescription for something that tasted exactly like, what else? Brandy. Out of the mouths of babes, I thought.

With her fever hovering around 103, I bundled the Princess back into the car and we headed to the drugstore before returning to the rest of our Christmas "vacation."

To tell the truth, the curse I had brought upon her had spread to me by this time and I was feeling increasingly lousy. I decided to get some Sudafed while I waited for the "brandy" bottle to be filled by a pharmacist who also looked younger than half the stuff in my medicine cabinet.

Oh, I got it. It was the day after Christmas. Everyone who had actually graduated from med school or pharmacy school was on vacation. We had been left to deal with the second string.

Whatever. Where was the damn Sudafed? And then I remembered that it's behind the counter these days. You have to show a picture I.D. and sign in before you can buy cold medicine because it contains pseudoephedrine, a fabulous decongestant that is a key ingredient in homemade methamphetamine. Think of it as the cream of mushroom soup of meth-making.

This is so unfair. Just because Meemaw has given up cooking chicken and pastry in the doublewide in favor of cooking up a big ol' batch of meth and biscuits, I get to be treated like some kind of *junkie* for trying to get a little cold relief?

Besides, you know what they say: When they outlaw Sudafed, only outlaws will have Sudafed.

I'm worried that it's going to get even harder to get the stuff. Will I have to prove that my cold is severe enough for Sudafed? Will I need a note from my parents? What if my watery eyes and red nose aren't good enough? Will I have to buy it in a dark alley behind the drugstore from someone named Knuckles?

I'm sure meth is a huge problem but I do wonder why so many towns seem almost eager to call themselves "The Meth Capital" of whatever state. The way they carry on about it, I expect it won't be long before you see it on city limits signs (Now With Even More Meth Labs Per Square Mile!). Will deputy sheriffs say, "You call yourself a meth capital? Don't make me laugh!"

Next year, I'm going to make more of an effort when it comes to Christmas.

And part of that is that I'm not going to call it "the holidays." Nope, I'm just going to call Christmas what it is. If anyone finds that offensive because it doesn't include any reference to their particular celebration of the season, if any, (and it is certainly their right not to celebrate anything at all although I should point out that there are some amazing prices on those circular diamond pendants along around late December), then that's just tough tinsel.

I'm weary of trying to be politically correct about Christmas.

This doesn't mean I'm anti-Semitic, anti-Muslim, anti-Buddhist, anti-Kwaanza, or anti-Perspirant.

While waiting for the "pharmacist" to fill our prescription, I remembered a funny thing that had happened the week before at a kid's birthday party.

Some of us were standing around talking about last-minute gifts we still had to buy, when one of the guests in our little circle stopped the conversation dead in its reindeer tracks with a terse, and rather loud, "I'm Buddhist."

I suppose this was her rather ham-handed way of reminding us that we were excluding her religion, which, up to this point, could've been the devout worship of Little Debbie Raisin Creme Pies for all I knew. They're cheap but soooo good so anything's possible, right?

And you know how some people do everything they can to avoid conflict because they're just Really Nice People?

And how others, meaning me, just feed off conflict like a roomful of cats on a week-old corpse?

Coupled with the sad fact that I'm not Really Nice at all is this awful personality defect that makes me crack a joke at the worst possible time.

What I should have said: "You're Buddhist? Oh, how interesting! I've never had the opportunity to learn about Buddhism. Please tell me more about your religion."

What I did say: "You're Buddhist? Wow! You don't look a thing like Richard Gere."

I know! Completely inappropriate but come on, a little funny, right?

Buddhist girl just sighed and walked away, presumably to find a quiet place in which to meditate about the ignoramus with the Little Debbie crumbs stuck to her sweater.

In December, people who don't celebrate Christmas must feel like the kid with the peanut allergy who has to eat lunch in the school library every day.

I do get it, and I'm sorry. But I ain't giving up my joy. Or my butterscotch haystack thingies.

18

How to Avoid Mortuary Science Camp

❧

Because I didn't just fall off the parental turnip truck, I'm now ready to share with those of you who may be new to this parenting thing, the single most valuable piece of advice that I could ever give you.

And, no, it's not that mushy stuff about how you should always make time for your kids because nobody ever says on their deathbed: "Gosh, I wish I'd spent more time at the office."

That's one of those things they really can't prove. It's just something that people say all the time, nodding sagely and acting like they just thought of it. But the truth is, who really knows? I mean, what if your kids are assholes? It happens. Maybe you really wish you had spent more time at the office.

So, no, I'm talking real wisdom, the useful shit. And here it is. Write it down somewhere, commit it to memory, do what you must but always remember these words:

> You must make sure to sign up your kids for summer camp by the end of March.

That's it. I know it sounds simple but you can plan to sign up your kid for camp, and then life and Pilates class and a random affair with the guy who grooms your poodle gets in the way and, before you know it, all the good camps are full and all that's left for your kid is "Yes, You *Can* Become a Mortician" and "Summer Fun with Actuarial Tables!"

Trust me. You have to jump on this camp stuff early or the only skills your kid will learn this summer will be how to Krazy-glue a cadaver's eyes shut or guess the exact day you're going to die and what's going to kill you. Neither of these is the kind of thing you want them practicing once they finish their week of camp and you're hanging out at the pool sipping mojitos with your grown-up friends.

("For the love of God, get your kid to stop talking about what he could do with my dead mouth and a jar full of cotton balls. It's cuh-reepy!") Your kid ends up going to loser-camps like that and he becomes Walking Buzz Kill.

Speaking of which, here's a true story: My mother-in-law

says that when my husband was three years old, he would count to 500 for any grown-up he could corner. He was scary-good at this and while the entire family was understandably proud of this prodigy-like behavior, I have to say that I feel nothing but pure empathy for the sap who got saddled with listening to a three-year-old recite "One hundred and eighty-nine, one hundred and ninety, one hundred and ninety-one . . ."

Still, it is famous family lore and everyone tells the story with great pride, including my husband (who, incidentally can now count all the way up to 600), but I just weep when I think about those poor, tortured souls who were cornered on the church steps or at the post office while he dutifully chirped "two hundred and twenty-one, two hundred and twenty-two, two hundred and twenty-three. Hey mister! Where you going? I'm not done yet!"

My point is that Walking Buzz Kill can start at an early age. You have to make sure your kid gets in the cool camps to avoid this horrible phenomenon.

Let me put this in terms you can understand: Summer camps are the lifeboat on the *Titanic* to a frazzled parent. You remember the movie, don't you? Let me spell it out for you: With summer camp, you're Kate Winslet, laying up there hogging the only piece of wood that's big enough to keep your fat ass afloat until help can come and cart you off to the big, warm boat where there will be blankets and hot tea.

Without summer camp, you're Leo DiCaprio, stuck with three-quarters of your body submerged in the frigid ocean water and your purple hands hands clinging to a tiny corner of that same piece of wood. Nobody's going to rescue your ass. And now you've got nothing left to do except wonder how long before your eyelashes frost over completely and you, finally, sink to certain death.

Scared yet?

If you've waited too late and everything, even mortuary science camp, is filled up, there is still a solution, sort of. You could be like my slacker friend, Barb, who has cagily enrolled her three kids in every Vacation Bible School in a seven-county radius. I don't approve of Barb's methods, but I have to admit that she knows how to make the best of a bad situation.

"Hmmmm," I said to Barb when she showed me a list of all the VBS locations she'd scheduled for the summer. "I didn't realize thee were Mennonite."

"Whatever it takes," she huffed back. "We're on a budget and this Bible School stuff is free."

"Yes, but you're not even religious, I mean, are you?" I asked.

"What difference does that make?" Barb snapped. "The snacks are killer and I've got three-plus-hours of free babysitting every day. If I play my cards right, which I will, I won't have to buy junk food for three whole months. The Presbyterians last year? They had *yogurt-covered pretzels* for snack one day. Do you have any idea how much those cost? My kids thought they were in heaven. So see, it really was a religious experience."

I must've looked horrified because Barb shot back: "Don't look so shocked. It's not like your kid isn't doing VBS."

"Yes, but just for *one* week and at my own church. You've got your kids going from Pentecostal Holiness to Episcopalian."

"I know," she said a little ruefully. "Last year, by the end of the summer, they didn't know whether to speak in tongues or demand wine with dinner."

"And don't you feel that you should give back a little?" I asked. "I don't want to get all sanctimonious on you, Barb, but you really should offer to help out at these things if you're going to send your kids to them."

"Oh, yeah? What are you going to be doing when your kid goes?"

"I'm doing the snacks one day."

"Oh, yeah? What're you bringing?"

"I'm making little tuna fish sandwiches and Goldfish crackers for Jonah and the Whale Day."

"Sandwiches? For real? Kids, get in here. There's been a change of plans. Y'all are going to be Methodists next week."

It didn't take long for Barb to figure out that about a third of the churches offer nighttime VBS.

I knew this but didn't tell her because I knew she'd enjoy it too much.

But when the Baptists hung a banner out front advertising nighttime VBS from six to nine, Barb couldn't believe her good fortune.

"You realize what this means?" she asked me one day.

"You can go to a movie with your husband and not have to pay a sitter?"

"Damn straight," she said. "Or out to dinner. We haven't done dinner or a movie since Ray Junior was born."

It was true. I kind of felt sorry for Barb because she told me the last movie she'd seen in the theater was *Men in Black* and that had been, like, a decade ago. She'd never even seen *Talladega Nights: The Ballad of Ricky Bobby*, which I consider a pure-T tragedy on account of it's the funniest movie ever. Every time I think about Will Ferrell jumping out of that car in his underpants, thinking he's on fire and screaming, "Help me Jesus! Help me Tom Cruise! Help me Oprah!" I just wonder to myself what the Academy is thinking when they ignore that kind of talent.

Instead, they always give the Oscar to somebody who made some incredibly depressing movie. When's the last time Hilary Swank made you laugh? I mean aside from that scene where she plays the boxer who gets paralyzed from the neck down and tries to kill herself by chewing her own tongue to pieces. Yeah, that one cracks me up every time.

With a script like *Million Dollar Baby* Pamela Anderson could have won the Best Actress Oscar.

And who was I to judge Barb, anyway? If the Lord helps those who help themselves, clearly Barb was doing the Lord's work.

Of course, some of my mom-friends have said that I shouldn't be worrying about day camps because it's time to send the Princess to (shudder) "sleep-away camp." Many of her friends have already done this for a couple of years, but I just can't stand the thought of my Precious spending weeks away from home.

"It's time," my friend Carol-Ann told me. "It will teach her how to be self-reliant. Sleep-away camp is fun for her and you, too. Think of all the quality time you'll have with your husband."

Yes, think of it. Four hundred twenty-six, four hundred twenty-seven, four hundred twenty-eight . . .

Carol-Ann wasn't giving up without a fight. Her daughter had been going to sleep-away horse camp for three years already and was training to compete in the Olympics.

"Yeah, what's up with that, anyway?" I asked. "Why doesn't the horse get the gold medal? He's doing all the work. Shouldn't he get the medal, a romp in the hay with a willing filly, and all the carrots and sugar cubes he can stand?"

"Don't change the subject," Carol-Ann said. "You just don't want to let go of your baby. I get that. But there comes a time in life where you have to love her enough to let her go."

OK, that's another dumbass thing to say like the thing about spending too much time at the office. Why does everyone talk like a Scholastic Book Fair poster these days?

Look, the only piece of parental wisdom you really need, I've already given you. The rest is just, well, Olympic-size horse poo.

Part III

It's Raining Men
(Must Be Why My Joints Ache)

19

Dancing with the Doofuses

❧

Maybe it's because I got hooked on watching *Dancing with the Stars*. Maybe it's because we've been married for nearly twenty years and the closest thing to a formal dance step hubby and I can do is the hokey pokey and sometimes even that doesn't work out because I forget to put my whole self in.

Whatever the reason, here we were, every Sunday afternoon, taking Beginning Ballroom Dance classes in a mirror-lined room alongside a dozen other jittery couples wearing "Hello" nametags.

In my mind, I would be Lisa Rinna to hubby's Harry Hamlin. We'd be good at this, possibly even great.

After all, didn't we have several decades' experience standing around with our eyes closed, swinging our heads from side to side during *Free Bird*? We had rhythm. Sort of.

The first class, hubby thought it would be hilarious to drape himself over me and grab my butt cheeks with both his hands in a little sentimental shout-out to the way everybody danced back in high school.

Unfortunately, I didn't know that's what he was doing and I just screeched, "What the hell is *wrong* with you, asshole? We're supposed to be having *fun*!"

The other couples looked at us funny. About half were our age, and half were young, fresh-faced engaged couples who wanted to look good for their wedding dance. So young, so wide-eyed and filled with love and understanding for one another. I could feel my lunch creep upward.

I wanted to mess with their sweet heads a little.

"Hey," I said to the bride-to-be who looked all of twenty years old. "What does it mean when your husband is in your bed, gasping for breath, and calling your name over and over?"

"I don't know, what?" she said, blushing and smiling.

"It means you didn't hold the pillow down long enough! Hahahahahahaha!"

"That's horrible!" she said.

"No, hon, horrible is when you realize that both of you have started ordering the pizza *before* you have sex because you know you'll be done way before twenty minutes and that way, there won't be any lag time."

"Well, that's not very romantic," said the bride-to-be.

"Romantic? Right. Get back to me the first time he asks you to 'see what you can squeeze outta that zit on my back' and here's the kicker! You'll *enjoy* it."

So far, between hubby's impromptu butt-cheek-grab and my sick sense of humor, we were zero for two as far as making friends with our Introduction to Beginning Ballroom Dance I for Beginners classmates.

While the perky marriage-minded couples were fun to watch, I felt more of a kinship with the elderly couple that fought all the time and always arrived with the distinct odor of bourbon wafting in the door behind them.

Dance-wise, things weren't going great. Along about week four, I felt ashamed that I had ever poked fun at Jerry Springer's spazzy turn on *Stars*. He was a *god* of dancing, a regular Mario López Baryshnikov compared to me.

The problem?

Our teacher, a wonderfully graceful woman who always appeared to float a couple of inches over the dance floor, took me aside and explained it simply: "My dear, you have a wobbly box."

Hubby's jaw dropped.

"I beg your pardon?" I said.

"A wobbly box," she repeated, not even attempting to lower her voice. "It's OK, dear, a lot of women have the same problem."

Oh, sweet Jesus, take me now on account of I'm fairly certain

I'm going to die of total and complete humiliation right this minute.

"Look," said hubby, suddenly feeling chivalrous. "I don't want to argue with an expert, but I simply have to say that my wife's box is not wobbly, not even close. And how would you know anyway?"

I looked at him with love-filled eyes. He was my hero, defending my, er, box.

"Because, dear," she said, looking directly at my husband. "I've been teaching dance for many years and when I see that someone's box step is a tad out of line, I just feel that I must try to correct it. You just can't go through these classes successfully with a wobbly box step."

Oh. We knew that.

"Gawd," I hissed at hubby. "What did you *think* she meant? You are such a perv sometimes."

Our teacher, too kind and innocent to even understand what had just transpired, patted my hand.

"You'll get it; it just takes time," she said. "You know it took me at least six months to learn the box step."

"Really?"

"Of course not."

A few minutes later, she selected hubby to demonstrate a new step, and I have to admit that now that he finally had a decent partner, he was dancing like John O' Freakin' Hurley.

Unfortunately, or perhaps because he was still smarting from the whole "perv" comment, this seemed to empower hubby to become the Family Dance Expert.

He began to orchestrate little impromptu practice sessions throughout the week.

"I'm honestly worried about your merengue," he said gravely one night.

"I'm honestly worried about your chances of living to attend the next class," I said.

The next Sunday, hubby practically fainted with pleasure when the instructor reminded us the male is always in charge and we must follow his lead at all times.

"Excuse me," I said, raising my hand. "You do realize that you're asking me to follow a man who gets lost driving to the mailbox, right?"

The truth was, I was having trouble making the transition from being our family's "decider" to following hubby's lead on the dance floor.

"Follow his core, dear!" the instructor would say as she magically appeared at my elbow like Tinkerbell, floating above the floor and whispering into my ear.

"You heard her," said hubby. "You're totally ignoring my core and stuff."

"Where is your core?" I asked.

"It's in the, er, esophageal area or perhaps the phalangeal area. Wherever it is, I've got one and you shouldn't be ignoring it."

And with that, he took me into his arms, pulled me close to his chest-core type space and, somehow, steered me into a perfect sequence of tricky rock steps.

He really was so much better at this dancing thing than

me. I could imagine *Stars'* Emmitt Smith voicing soft approval: "You're the big easy now, dawg" he would say to my husband.

With his new fancy-dancer status, hubby was really getting to be a bit of a handful around the house. We'd been at it for ten weeks and, while my box no longer wobbled, it was obvious that hubby was the dance talent in our household.

Which is why I didn't want him to see the newspaper article that reported that tall people are smarter.

His ego was already getting out of control.

I hid the morning paper in the dishwasher, the one place I was sure he'd never find it.

"Hmmm," he said, holding the curiously soggy newspaper that he had found (!) as he lowered his 6-foot-4-inch self into a chair meant for a much dumber person.

"It says here that Princeton researchers have discovered that tall people have advanced verbal and numerical skills," he crowed.

"That's ridiculous," I managed. "What about Yoda? He's really wise."

"He's a character in a *movie*," hubby said with obvious, high I.Q.'d impatience. "I'm talking about real people, like, say, *me*!"

"Oh, great," I pouted. "I knew you were going to get a lot of acreage out of this just because I'm only five-three."

He gave me an icy I'm-better'n-you look. And where did he get that damned smoking jacket? "You mean mileage, don't you? Not acreage. I know that expression because I am tall."

Damn this report published by the National Bureau of Economic Research (motto: "Tall but Unlaid").

"It says here that taller children as young as three perform significantly better on cognitive tests," said hubby. "You do know what I mean when I say 'cognitive,' don't you?"

"Don't make me hurt you."

"It's the process of using knowledge in the broadest sense," he said. "This includes perception, memory, judgment, the whole, if you will, enchilada."

"Sorry but I'm too short to understand all but the enchilada part of what you just said," I said, sarcasm dripping from my words like, well, something that drips a lot.

For some reason, ever since hubby had discovered the smart-tall connection, I was feeling shorter and dumber by the second.

"There are plenty of people who are tall but not smart," I said, while fervently trying to find my mouth with a forkful of peas. Tricky pea bastards.

"No, not really," said hubby. "Think about it. We've got Abraham Lincoln; you've got Tom Cruise."

Zing!

This must be how Pluto felt. You go through your whole life feeing like a pretty good planet, worthy of textbook illustrations and pop quizzes and cute little planet jingles to help everyone remember the correct order from the sun—My Very Excellent Mother Just Sent Us Nine Pizzas—and then you realize you'll never be pizza again. Or much of anything else except an oversized gas bag.

Speaking of which, there was hubby again, still crowing about his height advantage.

That night, he suggested we should go see *An Inconvenient Truth* but I wanted to see *Big Momma's House 2* instead. Hmmm. Two hours of Al Gore earnestly yammering about melting ice caps versus Martin Lawrence going undercover as an old fat lady to kick some terrorist ass. Talk about your no-brainer.

My self-esteem was taking a beating, though. I was short and therefore not smart *and* my fox-trot looked more like the frothy lunging movements of a rabid wolf.

As if all this wasn't enough, hubby came home one day showing me an article he'd seen about how Leos are better drivers. As in the ass-trological sign, not as in DiCaprio.

Leos, of which duh-hubby is one, are the best drivers on the road according to a new study, although I'm not sure it's right.

Wasn't this the same man who had borrowed my car recently and returned it with a missing side mirror because he hit an *ambulance*?

"Well," he pouted. "That ambulance was asking for it."

As a Virgo, I was curious to see where I stood. After all, Virgos are known for uncommon wisdom and restraint in all matters except perhaps the reading of *Soap Opera Digest* and eating fried pickles with ranch dressing.

Turns out Virgos ranked fourth. Not bad, but not great. Libras were the worst, by the way.

What does it all mean?

Well, as we all know, the auto insurance industry is forever on the lookout for ways to ensure that its clients are paying the lowest possible premiums, so you should probably bring the study to the attention of your agent the next time you're up for renewal. I'm sure the agent will hasten to reduce your policy rates unless he has choked on his own laughter and dropped dead. Then again, if you're a Libra, you might want to lay low and hope the insurance company never finds out or you'll wind up driving one of those little wind-up bikes beside the highway with all the drunk losers.

Our daughter's a Gemini, which was second best, and I'm relieved, even though she's still eight years away from getting her license. However she will never be allowed to ride with Libras (duh) or the other signs in the bottom three, Aries and Aquarius. She also won't be allowed to ride with Scorpio men because everyone knows they have just one thing on their mind.

In the meantime, hubby was convinced he was superior for another reason: He had gotten very, very good at Sudoku. An evil temptress, the cheap little tart, flimsy and soulless as paper, was stealing his heart every single night as we climbed into bed.

Who knew that "Sudoku" was Japanese for "You're not getting laid again."

Men can't resist these "wordless crosswords" that act as kryptonite to the entire Victoria's Secret inventory.

At least I know I'm not alone.

My friend, Susie, said she emerged from the bathroom recently trailing the scent of luscious bath oils and wearing a new black chemise. There was passion in her eyes as she walked toward the bed and saw her hubby, Fred, fretfully erasing and muttering.

"Honey?" she purred softly. "How do you like my outfit?"

Fred looked up for a second, grunted distractedly, and returned to his puzzle. "In a minute," he said. "I can't believe I didn't see that eight. What was I thinking?"

Yes, Fred, what *were* you thinking?

Frankly, Southern women don't know how to fight the Sudoku slut. We're usually quite gifted at dispatching man-encroaching hoochies to the four winds but *this*?

To be fair, which I just hate, we may have been doing some ignoring our own selves. Did we not just say no when Lifetime premiered *The Mermaid Chair*? But this was Kim Basinger seducing a priest while her crazy mama hovered in the background and chopped off her own fingers one by one! Surely we get a pass for that.

To be rejected for a bunch of blank squares just seems wrong. Still, I guess I understand.

Sudoku lures men away from us with promises of being "light and easy," qualities any thinking male absolutely loves. But then they better beware. Next is "demanding" and, finally, Sudoku becomes "very challenging."

Oh, sure, Sudoku is all "beer and ballgames are fun!" at first but watch out, guys. Before long, there are three numbers where there were once six already filled out and, next thing you know, it's "Mama's coming to live with us and I need me a Lexus and I signed us up for ballroom dance lessons starting next week."

Don't say I didn't warn you.

20

Gay Men Love Me

Hons, there's something about me that you should know: I don't like to brag, but gay men love me.

I mean *love me*. I'm like the poor (gay) man's Liza Minnelli or Barbra Streisand. OK, the very poor man's version, but you get the idea.

I've been a magnet for gay men for as long as I can remember and I have to say that I adore them right back. That said, there's something I don't get about straight guys: Why are y'all so threatened by gay men? They're not going to bother you because, frankly, have you even looked at your ratty-ass cuticles lately?

As a Friend to All Gay Men I've Ever Met (and thanks, by

the way, Fernando, for telling me about Spanx. If I was younger and unmarried, I swear I'd have one of those turkey-baster babies with you), I'd just like to say that my one community college psychology course taught me that when people yammer all the time about how they hate somebody else's lifestyle, it may be because they're secretly attracted to it.

Remember the Reverend Ted Haggard? He was a famous gay-basher who, it turned out, oopsie daisy, had engaged in repeated amorous encounters with a gay prostitute. This didn't come out until the gay prostitute saw Haggard on the news one night giving one of his famous anti-gay tirades and dude was big-time "WTF?" So, he alerted the media and Haggard finally confessed to a lapse in his normal completely heterosexual wife-and-kids-and-steak-every-Friday-night lifestyle in exchange for some mind-blowing moonie goonie with the male prostitute.

Not to worry, though. After three weeks of "intense counseling" Haggard was pronounced cured and "completely heterosexual."

I imagine gay men everywhere breathing a sigh of relief at that.

So what does a "reformed" gay man do when he gets "cured"? In Haggard's case, he announced that he was going to pursue his master's degree in psychology.

Isn't that just the most arrogant thing you've ever heard? He gets "un-gay" in three weeks (which, incidentally, is one whole week less than it took Sandra Bullock to kick Val-yum in the movie *28 Days*) and he's ready to tell the rest of us how to live.

Psychology? I'm thinking Midas Muffler School might be a better fit. Rev, read all the psychology books you want to while you're eating that ham and cheese sandwich at your desk between (ahem) lube jobs, but don't try to work on our heads. You think that you can go from gay to straight in twenty-one days, so that tells me right away that you're Unabomber levels of crazy.

Gay men must get mighty tired of sanctimonious blowhards like Haggard putting them down and telling them it's their choice to be gay and just snap the hell out of it.

Even when a straight man tries to sound all magnanimous and enlightened, it can backfire. Case in point: Shavlik Randolph, the NBA player who said it would be OK, sort of, for a gay pro basketball player to come out.

"As long as you don't bring your gayness on me, I'm fine," he said.

Sure, don't bring your gayness but could ya maybe bring some of that fabulous potato salad that you brought to the season opener cookout?

Bring your gayness on me?

Still, at least Randolph doesn't claim to speak for anyone other than himself. Like most heterosexual men, he's completely freaked out by gay men and he admits it. He might want to dig a little deeper as to why he's threatened by them but that's his business.

The king of sanctimony has to be the Reverend James Dobson, whose *Focus on the* (Not Gay!) *Family* series has millions of followers.

Dobson hates gays like Southerners hate toll roads. You could almost say it's an obsession.

After all, it was Dobson who first pointed out that there was a distinct possibility that SpongeBob SquarePants is gay.

Yes, the cartoon character.

In the words of SpongeBob's long-suffering coworker Squidward, "Oh, my aching tentacles."

Dobson is the chronically humor-impaired spokesman for the Christian right. That's how I know he wasn't joking when he told a roomful of rich supporters that SpongeBob appeared in a "pro-homosexual video" along with other known cartoon deviants including Barney the dinosaur (duh, he's gay because he's purple) and Jimmy Neutron, who, while not purple *is* highly intelligent and therefore suspect.

Dobson said that the video would be watched by millions of elementary school students and includes a reference to being "tolerant of differences." The nerve! Who does SpongeBob think he is? Jesus Christ? Tolerance will not be, uh, tolerated. Oh, and tolerance is quite possibly closely connected to gayance.

As a longtime Methodist Sunday School teacher and a huge fan of Mr. SquarePants, I'm uniquely qualified to say that, having watched every single episode, I see nothing un-Christian in the lifestyle of Bikini Bottom's most famous resident.

In contrast, SpongeBob consistently puts others first and returns good for evil. He turns the other cheek time and again to his miserly and cruel boss, Mr. Krabs, and has even made heroic efforts to befriend the very unlovable Plankton, the Zaccheus of the undersea world, as it were.

I can see why Dobson would dislike SpongeBob, though. His best friend is a *pink* starfish named Patrick (what a gay name!) and sometimes they even walk and skip arm in arm.

Dr. Dobson, as Aunt Ovaleen used to say when the Sunday sermon hit a little too close to home, you've done gone from preachin' into meddlin'.

If you persist in tarnishing the good name of the gentle-spirited, yea, Christ-like, SpongeBob, it will be obvious that you're the one who must live in a pineapple under the sea. With your head firmly planted in the sand

Besides, it doesn't take gaydar to know that SpongeBob isn't gay. He wears a short-sleeved shirt with a clip-on tie, for God's sake. No gay man alive would wear that frighteningly tacky combo.

To be honest, I prefer to deal with men who are straight or gay and comfortable with that. It's the mishmashy metrosexual that I don't get. That's why I was glad to read that the era of this famously *Details* reading, Abercrombie-on-the-weekend wearin', sushi-lovin', orchid-growing man-hybrid is finally, mercifully over.

Of course, hubby missed the whole metrosexual movement for lack of interest.

When we visited the cosmetics wonderland that is Ulta, I noted the huge section of skin and hair products just for men. In contrast, hubby noted that the Barnes & Noble across the street would probably have the newest fantasy league baseball magazine and he ran out of there like his clothes were on fire.

Here's a refresher for those of you who don't understand fantasy league baseball. This is when you draft real players for your pretend team and then your pretend team plays with other pretend teams and, when the real season is over, you see where your pretend team ranks and you celebrate by going out with all the other guys to buy really top-drawer exfoliating products.

Kidding!

But, like I say, I was always kind of underwhelmed with the whole metrosexual thing. Be gay; be straight; but for God's sake, pick one.

I don't like men who flirt with women in the arugula section while softly bitching about the declining quality of their favorite Chilean merlot.

Metrosexual dads wear me out, too. They're the ones at the playground who loudly brag about the "just a mere hint of asiago" they use in their homemade salad dressing to entice little Audubon to eat more veggies.

"Man up!" is the new battle cry and men are urged to eat hamburgers dripping with Paris Hilton and avoid toasting beers at the top because that's too much like man-kissing and similar rubbish.

As you can see, it's hard to get the balance just right. I say: Be gay if you're gay; be straight if you're straight.

From a perfectly selfish point of view, I'm glad to see the end of the metrosexual man because they always made me feel a little guilty. Their skin was smoother and it irked me to hear them carping about sheets with low thread counts.

"Go change some oil!" I wanted to shriek every time one of them sidled up to me at a picnic and wanted to discuss the latest Oprah book club pick with me. You don't like Nicholas Sparks so don't pretend you do, asshole.

In contrast, if gay men want to talk about the best French coffee press or debate whether tilapia is the new monkfish, I'm all in. But metrosexuals? What is that?

Ultimately, even the metrosexuals grew weary with all that forced shaving, sharing, and shopping. Turns out they really don't give much of a shit about which of the hand-painted porcelain drawer pulls at Restoration Hardware makes the boldest statement on the armoire, so stop the hell asking them.

As for hubby, he never knew what he missed. He's the kind of guy who would just assume that "Asiago" was a little-known left-handed reliever throwing in the Dominican leagues.

While I'm not sure exactly when metrosexuals just stopped, it may have been when they sauntered by one of those new Hooters-style barbershops like Bikini Cuts, where scantily clad women cut your hair and are even trained to make "sports small talk" with male customers.

As in, "Sooooo, how about that Boise State?" coos the leggy stylist with the rambunctious rack.

Yeah, girls can say stuff like "rack," too.

One of these chains brags that you can sit in a "state of the art" massage chair and catch the latest "flicks."

OK, your cool quotient is as nonexistent as Ann Coulter's

conscience. Flicks? I haven't heard that slang word for movies since *The Smurfs* went off the air.

At Bikini Cuts in Salt Lake City, you can even check out your stylist on-line. The girls, all wearing the equivalent of three Chinet cocktail napkins, have a wide range of interests. A typical profile promised that the stylist liked old people, vanilla lattes, and Mel Gibson movies.

Just call 'em *girls gone mild!!*

These manly barbershops would never have been acceptable to the metrosexual, who would peevishly carp about how they objectify women of which his mother and sister happen to be one. But those days are gone.

The naughty barber shops provide an opportunity for manly bonding in a comfortable way. In other words, not quite sharing ranch-hand duties in a pup tent at Brokeback Mountain but more in a "Whoa, check out the calzones on Misty Sue" kind of way.

I thought about all this stuff—the gay, the straight, the metrosexual, the calzones—while I waited for my eighty-four-year-old father to get his hair trimmed at Great Clips. Everyone kept their clothes on and I thanked God for it.

There was no sports talk, only four other men of varying ages discussing their back problems.

And none of them knew diddly-squat about asiago.

21

Penguins, Sir Paul, Rednecks

Unlucky in Love

⌇

Even though about half of all U.S. marriages end in divorce, people keep getting married. I figure that's because we Americans are, by nature, hopeful creatures. Our marriage won't fail; that's for other people.

So we have engagement parties and bridal showers and a registry at Target and never once do we imagine that we could be the couple that ends up separated in less than a year and squabbling over who's got custody of the waffle-stick maker.

Lately, technology has taken the place of the annoying first cousin matchmaker in the family and, on the surface, eHarmony and the rest seem to make a lot of sense. At least with "29 Dimensions of Compatibility" you've got a fighting chance, it would seem. With eHarmony, for instance, you are matched with someone who's a lot like you, almost scarily so. But it's not like when Eddie Van Halen married Valerie Bertinelli or Mick married Bianca because *she looked exactly like him* because that was all about the physical stuff. With eHarmony, they ask hundreds of highly specific questions. It's deep, y'all.

And while some people sniff at this, preferring to believe in the romantic notion that "opposites attract," I have to think that eHarmony founder Dr. Neil Clark Warren may be on to something.

I know three couples who are happily married after meeting through eHarmony. Their apparent success would seem to indicate that the compatibility thing works, especially if you're in it for the long haul and not just a few frisky moments of sparks-flying, toe-curling sex.

But, as my friend, Maybelline, complained after trying a few on-line dating services unsuccessfully: "There ain't nothing out there for the rednecks."

Of which she is one, in case you hadn't figured that out yet.

Maybelline is a terrific woman, but listing one of her "unique attributes" as the "ability to pee off the side of my daddy's bass boat while standing" wasn't the sort of thing most on-line dating services could really appreciate.

As I told Maybelline, if she had toned this down to simply

"I enjoy fishing and urinating at the same time" it might have sounded a little better.

Then again, maybe not.

Unlike Dr. Warren, I don't own a soothing voice or a gray suit, but I do know how to match-make a redneck.

At my redneckharmony.com, you would be eliminated or accepted based on my (sort of) patented "10 Dimensions of Compatibility" which I would call "What Y'all Got in Common." Rednecks need to feel the love, too, right?

Here's a sample of questions.

1. Have you ever given birth on a pool table? If so, how many times?
2. Have you, or any member of your immediate family, ever tried to remove a tattoo with eighty-grit sandpaper? From the baby?
3. Have you ever burned all the hair off your body while demonstrating the power of methane gas?
4. Have you ever tried to pay for a twelve-pack at the Stop-n-Rob convenience store using your mama's gold tooth? If yes, did you take it while she was passed out or ask her nice-like for it?
5. Have you ever stayed up all night building a beer bong for your little sister's eighth birthday present?
6. Have you ever heard yourself say, "While I admire the lilting oboe duet in Mendelssohn's Symphony No. 5 in D

Minor, I have to say that the andante of the final movement is what truly stirs my soul"?

7. Have you ever attended a cockfight? With a date? That
wasn't your sister?

8. Have you ever gone to the bank and applied for a loan
so you could get spinners and nekkid-lady mudflaps put
on your Gremlin?

9. Have you ever complained to a waiter that, while bleu
might be an acceptable substitute for gorgonzola crum-
bles in his universe, it most assuredly is not in yours?

10. Have you openly mourned the fading popularity of the
mullet hairstyle?

If you answered "Yes" to all but questions six and nine,
you will find your mate at redneckharmony.com. I had to add
those two weird questions to weed out the riff-raff, you know.

Happy redneck couples, don't thank me now; just thank me
by promising to get all the young'uns vaccinated, you hear?

Services like eHarmony could've saved Sir Paul McCartney
a lot of heartache.

While I'm not exactly ready to sponsor a telethon for Paul,
I do feel sorry for him. If you took away the billions of dollars,
the song royalties in perpetuity, and the still-irrationally-cute-
at-sixty-something looks, you'd have just another old guy that
got hoo-doo'ed by a one-legged heifer.

Happens all the time.

I predicted this breakup a long time ago, of course. You could see that marrying a woman that Paul's relatives early-on dubbed "an opportunistic cow" was doomed.

It's almost too easy to track poor Paul's marital woes the second time around via his greatest hits.

Some people see the Virgin Mary's face in a puddle of grits; I see that the songs foretold the whole sorry story. And, yes, it is a gift.

It was a remarkably brief journey from "I Want to Hold Your Hand" to "Help!" in Paul's case.

Asked how things are going, Paul says "I Feel Fine" but there's no longer any hope that "We Can Work It Out." Paul has discovered that while it's true that "All You Need Is Love," if your wife doesn't feel the same way, you're in for "A Hard Day's Night."

"Maybe I'm Amazed" that Paul couldn't just "Let It Be" and cherish the memory of his true soulmate, Linda. But he wanted "No More Lonely Nights" and so he penned a few more "Silly Love Songs" for Heather and proclaimed her to be "My (New) Love."

It is, after all, "Another Day," and when someone knocks on the door of your tattered heart, sometimes you just have to "Let 'Em In."

The British need their very own on-line dating services just for the Royal Family because, clearly, they have no idea how to pick the right spouse.

Look at poor ol' Camilla Parker Bowles. It took her years to drag Chuck to the church.

When Prince Charles finally agreed to marry his longtime shackmate, he decided the wedding would take place at Windsor Castle, but then he found out that if they got married there, they'd have to open up the ceremony to "commoners," which is the delightfully infuriating name the monarchy has for everybody else.

Charles and Camilla had a fallback plan and decided to move the wedding to Windsor Guildhall, described by Brits as "a quite handsome building." Sadly, they discovered they'd have to pare the royal guest list from 700 to just 100 because the Guildhall, while handsome, was too small. Rather like the late Dudley Moore.

Not only that, but the Guildhall, a public building, couldn't legally be closed to those pesky commoners either. So, it was entirely possible that the Duke and Duchess of Upper Monrovia and Lower Intestine would be seated beside some scurvy bloke eating salted mutton from a grease-spotted paper sack and staring at the royal nuptials like they were hotel porn.

As if that wasn't a big enough hassle, Chuck and Camilla couldn't legally marry until the Prime Minister passed a bill saying it was OK. And you thought it was a big deal when you had trouble matching the reception punch to your bridesmaids' dresses?

While Chuck and Camilla fretted about seating charts (should Lord and Lady Aspic be seated beside sour stick figure "Posh" Spice?), the Queen took a pass on the whole ceremony in favor of attending a private "blessing" ceremony.

I didn't blame her a bit.

"Y'all know me," she told the BBC while stabbing at her gums with a toothpick. "With me, it's all about the cake. Besides, I'd really rather stay home, soak my achin' dogs, and watch the race cuz *Dale Junior rocks!*"

Oh, no, she did-unt.

Well, of course not. But my redneckharmony.com clients would be able to relate to that little scenario.

I see a world of possibilities for franchising my idea of highly specialized matrimony Web sites. Even the animal world could benefit.

After seeing the fabulous *March of the Penguins* a while back, I was struck by the parallels between human and penguin relationships.

When the female penguin seems to be a little late returning from a food-finding mission while the males have been keeping the egg warm for four months (despite forty-seven-degrees-below-zero temperatures) the mood is, shall we say tense?

Rather like when we've gone to the mall and they're left with three kids and the cable's out.

In the movie, the males huddle, and although I'm not fluent in penguin, I'm fairly certain that after multiple home viewings of this movie I can interpret some of the chirps and screeches thusly:

1st male penguin: "Where are the girls? We're gotta go get some food soon!"

2nd male penguin: "Dude, I feel ya. Women have no freaking concept of time. I sure could go for some nachos about now."

1st male penguin: "What are nachos?"

2nd male penguin: "I dunno, but I saw Morgan Freeman eating some with the crew the other day. Wait. I hear something! It's the girls! They're back! Here they come! Sweetheart! Where have you been for four months? Long time, no see. Here's the kid. I'm outta here. Love ya, mean it."

Female penguin: "Oh, so it's like that? I get back after walking and sliding on my belly for four months just so I can eat enough to get back here and throw up into Junior's gullet *so he will live* and all I get from my (makes little quote marks in the air with her flippers) lifetime mate, is this? That is just *so* typical of you."

2nd male penguin: "Okay, let me get this straight. I'm out here for four months freezing my mukluks off, protecting our kid, surrounded by a bunch of guys that *look exactly alike* and you act like it's been a party."

Female penguin: "By the way, that whole penguins-always-mate-for-life thing that you fed me and I swallowed like regurgitated cod, turns out, isn't true. The girls and I were talking about that while we were walking *seventy miles back* from trying to find food."

2nd male penguin: "Doris, honey, I never said 'for life.' Everbody knows we penguins are mates for a year, two at the most. Life goes on."

Female penguin: "MY NAME'S NOT DORIS!"

2nd male penguin: "Uhhh, Mabel?"

Female penguin: "Wrong again, tuxedo-face."

2nd male penguin: "C'mon, I've kept the kid warm but he's hungry. So instead of giving me grief, let's think about his needs first, shall we?"

Female penguin: "Why you sanctimonious squid-sucker! I oughta . . ."

Over the years, I've heard other women joke that what they really need isn't a husband at all. What they really need is a wife.

Now that I've watched HBO's *Big Love* series about a Utah polygamist, I get it.

Three women share this very ordinary-looking and bizarrely earnest owner of a home-improvement store and they happily live in a suburban "complex" with a shared backyard.

Although there are three wives, it's the first one who has the "biggest love" so to speak. She's the alpha-wife, just like I would be. The "sister-wives," as the second and third are called, share second-place affections.

But back to why I need a wife.

On *Big Love*, having extra wives makes for a lot less house-work. You cook only every third night, if at all. Some of the wives seem to be conveniently absent during much of the meal preparation. There are so many kids that you always have built-in baby-sitters hanging around wearing those ghastly '80s hair combs and beatific smiles.

Plus, two nights out of three, there's virtually no chance that you'll be forced to switch from *The Daily Show* to *Sports-Center*.

Perks, perks, everywhere!

So I asked duh-hubby how he'd feel about having an extra wife or two around here and he lit up like the time I told him *MacGyver* had finally come out on DVD.

"No, no, no, don't get the wrong idea," I said. "Just some extra wives to help with chores and tend the Princess."

"Where's *MacGyver*?" he asked sulkily.

Mormons hate *Big Love* because they're scared it's going to get us riled up about the image of eighty-year-old pervs marrying fourteen-year-old girls, but I don't think they should worry.

We know Mormons don't do that stuff anymore, except for a few inbred nut-jobs that splintered off to cult-land and live in caves without cable or Starbuck's so we know they're all crazy.

Much to the frustration of the Mormons, polygamists tend to hang out in Utah. You won't ever hear about any polyga-mists in the South because Southern women don't share any-thing.

You honestly believe a Southern woman is going to share her duh-hubby in the sack when she won't even share her recipe for chicken salad? Oh, hell no.

Billy Bob will never have five mommies. Southern women are notoriously territorial when it comes to circling and spraying around our men. He might be the sorriest excuse for a husband that God ever created, but he's "our'n" and just cause he wears a paper hat at work and drives a drunk bike, it doesn't make any never-mind. If another woman so much as looks at our husband, we will tighten our grip on his arm like a python squeezing a live chicken.

Truthfully, I couldn't be one of many wives because I prefer to nag and belittle one man at a time. Besides, I'd look like shit in a prairie skirt.

22

Don't Bug Me, I'm Reading "The Little Red Hen"

❧

Every time somebody introduces a new study that reveals something about men, I'm all in. Anything that can shed even a tiny ray of light on how men think is fascinating to me.

That's why I was so excited to read the results of a new study revealing cavemen preferred blondes.

According to the British science journal *Evolution and Human Behavior*, ground-breaking research now proves that, during the Ice Age, Northern European cavewomen so outnumbered cavemen that the men could have their pick of mates. And they picked blondes!

You see, cavemen were responsible for hunting for food and often they didn't survive the hunt. So, as their numbers began to seriously dwindle, the cavewomen who had been left behind to tend the cave and carp about their insensitive spouses found themselves on the horns of a wooly mammoth, I mean, dilemma.

Obviously, if the cavewoman didn't have a man, there would be no mastodon casserole that night and, eventually, these mate-less cavewomen would die alone, hungry and, worst of all, brunette.

So nature and evolution combined to give some of the more fortunate cavewomen a caveman-attracting makeover: A new look of blond hair and blue eyes began to emerge and four out of five cavemen polled by Fox News (still the favorite of cavemen everywhere) apparently said, "Me likey."

Before too long, the journal reports, the dark-haired cavewomen, the un-evolved you might say, began to hiss and snipe behind the blond cavewoman's back calling her "Jessica Simpson" and other insulting names.

Scientists explained that when an individual is faced with potential mates of equal value, each carrying identical quantities of twelve-packs and hot wings, he will tend to select the one that stands out in a crowd.

The British study was backed up by a Japanese science journal that reported the gene responsible for blond hair appeared for the first time about 11,000 years ago or, I like to think, when cavewoman finally discovered Preference by L'Oréal because she was worth it.

I'm guessing it didn't take long before the first blonde jokes began to surface, most likely at book club meetings organized by the smarty-pants brunette cavewomen.

Brunette cavewoman to blond cavewoman: "This month's selection is *Crime and Punishment* by Fyodor Dostoyevsky. But, since this might prove a bit challenging for you, Blondie, you can start with, let's see, yes, here it is, *The Little Red Hen*. I hear it's *fascinating!*"

While researching all of this I discovered an article quoting the World Health Organization (motto: "Smoke 'em if you got 'em"), saying that natural blondes are likely to be extinct within 200 years because fewer people are carrying the blond gene. In fact, the WHO has predicted the last natural blonde will probably be born in Finland in 2202. And she will be *really* stacked.

Kidding! That WHO thing turned out to not even be true! Oh, those WHO cutups and their hoaxes! Maybe they're just jerking our chains over the whole Bird Flu pandemic thing, too. If so, I believe I speak for all good rednecks when I say, "I call gizzard!"

Hey, don't judge. Gizzards rock!

The thing I've noticed lately is that it's the brunettes who are doing the really nutty stuff most of the time. Two examples: Jennifer Wilbanks, (see: "Fifteen minutes of fame, comma, outlived") the bug-eyed "runaway bride" from Georgia who faked her own kidnapping just to get out of her wedding. I think she probably came undone when it dawned on her that she would have to greet 600 wedding guests in a receiving line without so much as a Jordan almond to munch on. And being a Southern girl, she knew she'd have to write hundreds of thank-you notes within two months of the wedding or die trying. Southern brides who are tardy in their thank-you notes are in grave danger of being labeled "tacky" by their Southern sisters, a dreaded adjective that is to be avoided as surely and swiftly as men who wear Birkenstocks and socks.

At first, I was blown away by the runaway bride's loyal fiancé who, even after seeing his beloved hiding beneath a striped beach towel and being led through a New Mexico airport on national TV, vowed to stick by her side. Stoic and devoted, he seemed to understand there are just some times in this life when that which is bitten off must also be chewed. Fortunately, he came to his senses eventually and dumped her scrawny ass. Now that was a man I could understand. That made sense.

Example two of brunettes gone psycho would have to be the poor lovesick space-lady Lisa Nowak. And while the rest of the world was aghast at her puzzling behavior, pepper-spraying her old boyfriend's new girlfriend in an airport parking lot after driving halfway across the country, I was more aghast that this woman, raised in the South, would ever drive fourteen hours straight anywhere.

It's true. The disguise, the pepper spray, the knife, the pills, the porn and, yes, even the fabulous space diapers, just made me sad. But the notion that she had renounced her Southern upbringing to the point of driving without so much as one night in a HoJo Express let me know right away she'd gone crazy. Southerners just don't do this. Not even the men.

A Southerner considers it a sacrifice to sit in a car longer than four hours. In contrast, everyone I've ever met from the North believes that stopping overnight is a sign of weakness. To hear my friend from Long Island talk, "all's you need to get to California is a couple of pee breaks and then just 'cause the kids are whining."

While both of those brunettes lost their men, maybe there's something to the notion that men, perhaps channeling the preferences of their caveman ancestors, will fight harder to get the blonde.

It's a fact: Men are easily manipulated by blondes and by their other great love, fast food.

The Hardee's/Carl's Jr. burger chain has made it clear that they're not interested in women or children as customers. Not only does Hardee's not offer a happy meal, they don't even offer a "merely content" or "borderline depression" meal for tots. Fair enough, but why alienate me? I've got spending power *and* bowel control.

Through an unapologetically misogynistic advertising campaign that is clearly geared to the "inner caveman," Hardee's has made it clear that they are interested in selling food to the manly man who can simultaneously change the tire on a big rig and scratch his naughties. As a modern-day woman, I can just take my mood swings and "salad-with-dressing-on-the-side" habit elsewhere. Please.

For a couple of years now, I've watched Hardee's commercials and print campaigns make one thing very clear: Real men who work on big engines in tight T-shirts and eat steroidal cheeseburgers believe that women are only good for looking pouty and handing them a wrench now and then. In one commercial, a gorgeous leggy blonde sighs meaningfully when her beau shows more interest in the burger than her.

If you ask me, dude needs a visit from the Cialis fairy if he actually prefers the "monster thickburger," a two-fisted meat-fest, to what is clearly presented as "a sure thing."

Size matters . . . to cavemen. Why else would we see Burger King telling men that what they really need is The Enormous Omelet.

Morgan Spurlock, who skewered McDonald's in *Super Size Me*, suggests the omelet sandwich should come with a five-bucks-off coupon for your first angioplasty.

Not to worry, men. I'll bet it will be a really *big* angioplasty. And with any luck at all, your surgeon will be a blonde.

23

Brownies and Men

They Both Have Nuts on 'Em

It amazes me that the very same duh-hubby who spends hours analyzing the earned run averages of long-dead baseball pitchers and comparing the ratios of pixels of whatever TV screen he's considering buying can come completely unglued at the prospect of ordering fast food for his family.

My hubby isn't alone in this. Like most women, my heart automatically sinks when I discover that I'm in line behind a dad with children at the fast-food drive-through.

The other day, I bat-turned my way into the drive-through at Crack-fil-a for what I hoped would be something quick and greasy. Just ahead of me in line was the sight that you never want to see if you're running late: a man, late thirties to early forties, driving his wife's Pacifica with one of those obnoxious rear window decals where the whole family, including the dog, cat, and bird are pictured in happy little white outlines like they were drawn by some chalk-wielding psychopath.

"Ha!" the smug decal seems to be saying. "Our family is happy and smiling and our life together is just one big, funny, happy cartoon of merriment! Even our animals are smiling, as you can see, because we are *so frikkin' happy*."

I think it would be funny to have one of those family decals showing a really skinny teenage girl barfing into a little chalk-outline bag (the bulimic in the family) or the dad figure dressed in the women's underwear that he truly enjoys slipping into when no one's looking. Or the wife figure smiling with her exaggerated curly hair and tennis skirt, clutching a racket in one hand and a bottle of Stoli' in the other.

Or the family cat, big smile on the face as usual, with just the lower third of the family parakeet's body protruding from his jaws. Now that's one big happy family!

All that forced family happiness just annoys the shit out of me but I was even more worried because I knew that this doofus dad would never get the order right. He would try, and it would break my heart to hear him, but he would never get it right.

(This is why, if there is a woman in the car, she will end up lying halfway across her duh-hubby's lap and screeching the correct order into the speaker herself.)

Men only speak one side and it is "fries." Do not confuse them with mandarin oranges or yogurt with live cultures unless they can be fried.

The drive-through was especially slow on this day, leading me to think that everyone ahead was a dad with children, no mom on board. As we inched forward, a sign with a smiling chicken on it informed me that, between 11 A.M. and 2 P.M. the day before, that very drive-through had served something like 2,362 people. And this is supposed to make me feel better because? . . .

Finally, Pacifica pulled up to order.

Here we go.

Men scream at drive-throughs so there was zero chance that I'd miss a second of the inevitable screw up.

"Uh, yeah. Gimme six number threes with Sprite."

Yeah, that's all he said.

There were kids in the car so it wasn't possible that the order could be that simple.

There was no mention of subbing the whole milk for Sprite for the youngest little chalk drawing or that all the kids required precisely eighteen different tubs of the four available sauces for their nuggets.

As if on cue, the chalk children began to bob up and down and howl and I watched the formerly confident dad sink into his seat and cover his ears.

"I said honey mustard SAUCE, not honey mustard! *I don't want honey mustard.* They're completely different. You don't even *know who I am!*"

One of the smaller chalk drawings flung a hissy fit for a nugget upgrade from the six-piece to the nine-piece because "*I am physically going to starve to death.*" The dad grabbed what appeared to be a paper sack and breathed into it.

Four agonizing minutes later, Pacifica Dad lurched forward but I knew this was far from over.

As he passed drinks back to the kids, I heard one of the chalk drawings scream: "*There's blood in my lemonade!*" Of course, moms know that it is, in fact, maraschino cherry juice because they use the same tongs for lemons as they do for the milk shake cherries. I toyed with the notion of getting out of my car and telling this to the hapless dad but it was more fun to sit and watch.

Lemonade "blood" was explained away by the drive-through lady to everyone's satisfaction and Pacifica Dad slowly pulled away. I was sure he forgot to order anything for himself so I gave him time. Sure enough, there were his back-up lights.

With a mix of contempt and pity, I watched him retrieve something for himself. He started ahead again but I still didn't pull up. Back-up lights again, as expected. He forgot the napkins. He finally pulled into an empty space, car engine running, and sprinted into the store, returning with straws, sporks, and a bag of brownies.

As the Pacifica finally pulled away for good, I heard the squeal I had been expecting. Another rookie mistake. "Oooooh, ick! *These have nuts on them!*"

Maybe because they're so traumatized by trying to order fast food for their children, men head for the hills when it's time to buy school supplies. This is also a task that involves a multitude of choices and the great possibility that you will get a royal ass-chewing from someone if you get it wrong.

At Open House at the Princess' elementary school this year, I couldn't help but notice the dads looked much more relaxed than the moms. They were having a rousing discussion about who had what brand of high-def TV and how many pixels it would take for the best viewing of *Sunrise Earth*. (Have you seen this? Our friends have practically quit their jobs to watch the sun rise in real time in high-def. One couple I know spent two hours transfixed by the sight of a moose emerging from a river and shaking dewy, high-def droplets off his, er, moose parts. What is with that?)

While the menfolk gathered to discuss how they spent three hours watching a hot-air balloon flight over New Zealand, I decided to pop into the girls' rest room to check my makeup.

But I had to bend down really low to see myself because apparently they put mirrors low enough for the kids to see themselves because *it's all about them*. Grown-ups just get a highly depressing reflection of their hips and thighs that can be very unsettling if you're not prepared for it. It's like how when you check into a hotel and you go to your room and the first thing you do is sit on the potty and you realize, to your horror, that the mirror is on the back of the door and now you have to *watch yourself take a dump.* . . . So you read a magazine but, every time you look up, there you are. In high-def.

Back in the girls' room, I stooped way down to check out my complexion. I looked tired, that much was true. Who could blame me? I'd spent the previous day school-shopping with the Princess. I'm not saying that men never do this; I'm just saying that they do this about as frequently as they TiVo the Paris runway shows on Bravo.

Shopping for school supplies always sounds like such a fun thing to do until you actually do it. You plan lunch around it, you get the Official Sanctioned Supply List from the school and you plan a fabulous day of mother-daughter bonding, Orange Juliuses and perhaps a sale trinket from the rounder at Limited Too.

The day starts well enough but fast-forward an hour or two and you're standing in the seventh circle of hell or, as I like to call it, Target, clutching a now-sweaty list that says you must have a one-inch binder, four non-college-ruled composition books, and plastic—not paper—homework folders.

The problem with this is twofold: kittens and Gwen Stefani. Those cute and cool looks are only on the wrong kind of paper or the wrong size binder. The ones that are on the approved list from the school look like something they'd let Scott Peterson write home on.

So we had a big ol' mother-daughter meltdown right there in the aisles of Target that ended with me screeching: "If you put that college-ruled 120 page composition book with the horsey on it in our cart, I swear I'm going to put back the Crayolas and we're going to Dollar Tree and buy the crappy crayons that leave oil stains all over your paper and have colors like 'phlegm.' "

We finally agreed to compromise. The Princess would get the Hannah Montana tissues for the class, but I was buying the generic hand sanitizer instead of Purell.

"That stuff probably doesn't work as well," she moaned. "I'll bet it doesn't even kill that many germs. There was a girl in my class last year who licked her arms all the way down from her elbows to her fingertips every day and the teacher made her use Purell."

Whoa. I didn't know Courtney Love was in my kid's class.

Of course, the real kicker is that none of it was necessary. Except perhaps the Orange Julius, on account of I believe that when it comes right down to it fluffy drinks made from imitation orange-flavored powder are one of the few things that separates us from the savages.

On the first day of school, we were handed a completely different list from the classroom teacher.

"But this says college-ruled, we thought it had to be non-college-ruled paper," I whined.

"It really doesn't matter, whatever you like," said the teacher, who was wearing some gauzy hippified dress made of hemp.

"Whatever I *like*? What about the one-inch binder? We went to six stores and couldn't find one."

"So get a two-inch one," she said smiling. "Or three or even four! Sometimes you just have to go with the flow!"

Had she been smoking her dress? What kind of public school teacher was this? Besides, the last thing I was in the mood for was some childless twenty-five-year-old telling me to go with the flow. Why did I know with utter certainty that she would have happy chalk outline drawings of her family on the back of her van in a few years?

"And plain red or blue? That was really hard to find," I kept on.

"Oh, I know!" she said. "But some of the students found these really cute notebooks with cats and even one with Gwen Stefani on it. Those are fine. Sometimes, you just have to . . ."

"Yes, I know, go with the flow."

"That's right!"

After Open House, we came home and duh-hubby got happily engrossed in watching a barely moving herd of buffalo wander tediously across the screen.

I realized that I could really go for a buffalo burger, but it didn't seem like the right time.

But then something strange happened. The scene switched to a waterfall and I was the one who couldn't look away. Gone was the frustration of school-shopping and waiting in line for idiot dads to order food at a drive-through. The picture seemed oddly familiar and then it hit me: It was just like watching those pictures they have on the walls of the nation's finer mediocre Chinese restaurants where one little part of the picture is moving, usually a waterfall or rushing river, and at first you're sure it's the off-brand sake you drank but then you realize the picture is honest-to-God moving. Like those eyes in the portraits on the wall when Scooby Doo is helping solve a mystery.

"It's so relaxing," said hubby, wrapped in his favorite pink blanket. "You can just feel the weight of the world lifted."

Looking at the beautiful waterfall and the peaceful face of my duh-hubby, I felt a strange tug of sentimentality. Maybe those sappy family outlines weren't so bad. Maybe I was just being harsh and judgmental. The peaceful feeling seemed to pervade all my senses and I could feel old knots relaxing in my neck and back. I felt as if I could sit here and watch this waterfall forever. And smoke that teacher's dress.

Why couldn't I be more like my husband, unruffled by life's daily annoyances? Why couldn't I be more like my daughter's teacher, with her soothing voice and uplifting attitude, even though it's beyond me how anybody can spend nearly seven hours a day with kids who start every sentence with "Guess what?" I mean every damn sentence out of their mouths.

"Guess what?"

"What?"

"I went to the zoo with my friend Mona and, guess what?"

"What?"

"We saw these weird little sheep and guess what?"

"What?"

You get the idea.

We watched the waterfall and it was so vivid, it was practically forming puddles on the floor below the TV screen.

I was liquid, completely calm, incapable of being upset by anything at all. Well, almost anything.

"Hey," said hubby, still staring at the waterfall. "Don't forget my sister's birthday's tomorrow. Better get something in the mail, OK?"

The knots returned immediately. Why can't a man buy his own sister a birthday present?

"Oh, just get her some lotion," he said, sensing that I was losing my waterfall calm and turning more into a boiling cauldron.

Lotion is the idiot-man's solution to every gift-giving dilemma.

Ask any woman. We've all got enough lotion in various drawers and cabinets to lubricate the entire membership of the Red Hat Society.

Of course some lotions are nice to receive: the kind that are sealed up really well so you can easily get the cash for them when you take them back to the store and get *something useful*.

And men, bless their hearts, don't know how to buy lotion. I don't want to smell like brownies or spice cookies or a rum toddy. Trust me; I'd rather have the real thing.

Giving lotion as the easy gift has managed to accomplish the impossible: It makes the Hickory Farms Beef Stick look good.

"Buy it yourself," I snapped. "She's *your* sister."

"Can't," he said simply, pulling the blanket tighter under his chin, never taking his eyes off the screen. "Tomorrow there's going to be a twelve-hour marathon on the purple martin migration. They're practically an endangered species, you know."

Yeah, I know. Not unlike a man who can order fastfood, buy school supplies, and buy his own sister a birthday gift.

Part IV

(I'm so Totally)
∽ Random Thoughts ∾

24

Latest Technology's All Geek to Me

❧

When you work from home, you tend to talk to the furniture. No, no. What I meant to say was that you tend to obsess over things that you wouldn't have time to worry about at the office.

Like how my Internet Service Provider (SOB) has started sticking stupid little advertisements at the bottom of every e-mail I send.

Let's just say that it's monumentally annoying to write a heartfelt e-mail to a friend in crisis only to realize that Big

Dumb Brother has added, "Want to learn how to send mail for free AND get videos from across the Web?"

Pretty soon, they'll be selling the space to that creepy widow in the unpronounceable country who wants to split her dead husband's vast oil well fortune with me just because.

Just yesterday, I was telling filing cabinet that I'm going to fight back. After all, they could put *anything* at the end of my e-mail ("Republicans Rock!") and I would have no control.

I decided to be Polly Proactive about the situation and I e-mailed my SOB to tell them I found this nasty little free advertising postscript extremely intrusive and to kindly stop doing this.

Now of course I realize how truly idiotic that was because, four auto-replies later, we're still nowhere, and I could swear lamp just giggled.

The company's response was obviously computerized because it had nothing to do with anything I wrote: "There is no problem with your computer or account! This is our way of sharing with our customers exciting new offers and services!"

Oh! Well then! Bite me!

Fortunately, they added, my input was valued and "very beneficial."

Oh, well, that's nice. No! That's not nice at all. They're just manipulating me into thinking they're nice.

The response continued, "Customer input is the best way we know to provide such great service."

Such great service? But this was a *complaint*! My brain hurt.

Finally, it got to the point: There is no possible way to delete the nasty little postscripts from my e-mail and their response for now and all time would be, essentially, tough toenails.

My second, third, and fourth e-mails ranged from simply shrill to potentially libelous. I figured that tougher language would ensure that I'd get a human to respond instead of the ever-more-annoying computer-generated mail. I even went so far as to warn that I should not be messed with because it just so happened that I was a famous book writer and a nationally syndicated columnist and they most certainly wouldn't like me to write about their abysmal customer "service" because tens or perhaps even dozens of people would possibly read it.

This, apparently, didn't exactly leave them shaking in their cyber boots.

The very next day, I got a generic e-mail from "Dallas" thanking me for "voicing concerns."

That was it.

I hate "Dallas" and the rest of the computerized response team. And, boy, if you think I'm mad about it, you should see desk calendar.

Despite our fight, my ISP, the SOB, continues to send me little reminders of how hard they're working to keep spam out of my life.

Before the Internet, there was only one kind of spam, that lumpy, gelatinous pink stuff that came in a can with a key. Which, now that I think about it, is just about the coolest thing imaginable: food that must be opened with a key. And the key would break off sometimes and you'd lose it and then you'd just have to settle for the Vienna sausages, which were neither sausage nor from Vienna, so go figure.

I figure spam—the Internet kind—must be a huge problem because I've been getting more of those messages that require me to fill out a form before the recipient will condescend to read the e-mail I've sent.

The message usually goes something like this: "I apologize for this automatic reply to your e-mail. To control spam, I now allow incoming messages only from senders I have approved beforehand. If you would like to be added to my list of approved senders, please complete the request form below. Once I approve you, I will receive your message in my inbox."

Oh, screw it. You're not worth all that trouble.

Once you *approve* it? Oh lah-dee-dah-dee-dah.

I don't know why this bugs me unless it's because I don't like being lumped into the category of potential spammers such as the long-winded pity-partying rich widow who so desperately wants to divide her immense fortune with me even though we've never met.

I also get frequent e-mails from a desperate deposed despot who wants to send me millions of dollars if I'll first send him a cashier's check to bail out a relative wrongly incarcerated in a some nasty Thai prison. Like I care.

It's nutty, I know, but I don't like the notion of being "approved" or "not approved." What if I'm not approved? Junior high all over again, that's what.

Another cyber trend that grates is the auto-reply. Let's say you send a warm, witty, and well-composed e-mail to an old friend. You hit "send" and in a matter of seconds, the friend has already replied.

So you open it but what's this? It's the friend's auto-reply saying that she is unavailable to read your e-mail. For reasons of vacation or a business trip or gum surgery, you will simply have to wait.

Well, OK. But where does my e-mail go in the meantime? To e-mail purgatory? Will it ever be read or will it float around in space, unseen, like yet another Jason Alexander sitcom?

I get that auto-reply is sent so you won't think the person is being rude by not acknowledging your e-mail, but I don't care. I want a real, live Darrin Stevens-on-*Bewitched*-type secretary to tell me that.

And who's to say auto-reply won't take over completely one day, protectively saying that you're out of the office when, in fact, you're sitting right there at your desk digesting that giant poppyseed muffin you just had to have?

After all, it's not such a stretch to think your e-mail will start lying for you when it's already adding intrusive little messages to your personal correspondence.

While I've become completely dependent on e-mail (don't tell my ISP, the SOB), it doesn't mean that I want it on my cell phone, which is something Precious and duh-hubby can't grasp.

My cell phone (gasp!) doesn't even take pictures.

Which is just as well because do we really need pictures of everything right away?

A friend brought her tiny new camera phone to dinner one night and tested it out on all of us.

"Look!" she squealed. "Here you are five seconds ago sitting right beside me! At least I think that's you. It's kinda hard to tell on these things."

She was right. It was either me or a very large and unappetizing block of parmigiano-reggiano.

"I'm going to e-mail this to everybody!" she said, punching a few more magic buttons.

While we waited for our dinner to arrive, she reviewed the 232 pictures she'd already taken on the phone, including several pictures of her toes.

"I got a pedicure," she gushed.

"I'll alert *Inside Edition*," I said snottily. Where the hell was my mojito?

The cell-phone picture show is a modern version of the '60s slide shows of the annoying neighbors' trip to visit the world's largest frying pan, or some such.

"And look here, this is Cammie Sue's birthday party last week."

OK, so, "A," I don't know Cammie Sue and "2," I don't care.

These camera phones bring out the worst in people. The other day, I was waiting in line at a restaurant when the guy ahead of me began to flex his gi-normous biceps.

"Welcome to the gun show!" he said. More like the mo-ron show, if you ask me.

While he posed and preened, a woman gleefully aimed her cell phone at him. For a happy moment, I didn't realize it was a phone and I thought she was trying to vaporize him but, sadly, she was just taking his picture and e-mailing it to her goofy-ass girlfriends.

Everybody has a phone with Internet access and a little camera built in and fabulous ring tones. Everyone except me.

When my daughter's nine-year-old friend's phone erupted with Justin Timberlake announcing that he was bringing sexy back, I said "Enough!"

This necessitated a painful-for-all-of-us lecture on How Music Has Gone into the Shitter Ever Since Along About 1987.

In the mall, cell phones buzz around me with Shakira's poetic message that "Lucky my breasts are small and humble, so you don't confuse them with mountains." Girl, who needs Maya Angelou?

And who can fail to mist up at Fergie's anthem: "My humps, my humps, my lovely lady lumps." Hmmm. "My lunch, my lunch, I swear it's coming up."

The Princess' friend changed her ring tone to something by John Mayer but even that was on the nasty side, I thought.

"I'll never let your head hit the bed without my hand behind it." What does he mean? The headboard? And, if so, that's just about the most unromantic thing I ever heard. Why not: "I will never leave the toilet seat up on account of you don't like it."

Still, I guess we can all be grateful that I haven't yet heard a ring tone for Diddy's delightful "Young, black and famous, with money hanging out the anus." I feel ya, Diddy. That's so beautiful it'd bring tears to a glass eye. Maya Angelou, I repeat, you are *toast*!

While I'll admit that I'm a tech dinosaur, what with my whinings about computers and cell phones, even I was shamed when the Princess asked me, with pretend innocence, if my cell phone came with its own booth.

OK, maybe it was time for an upgrade. But I swear I will not be one of those tacky people who are forever taking pictures with the thing. Celebrities have zero privacy thanks to this cell-phone stalking that goes on.

You just never know who's going to snap your picture and splatter it like bird shit all over the Internet. Just ask Kate Moss, if you can get her head out of that big old bag o' blow, that is.

25

It's No "Secret"

How *TV Guide* Ruined My Life

❧

Hons, it's a sad moment when you realize that your true calling, the reason you were put here on God's green earth, will always elude you.

I refer, of course, to my dream of being the person who writes the program descriptions for *TV Guide*.

The dream died in the year of our Lord two thousand aught six when my beloved periodical, that which hath served as coaster to many a sweaty glass of iced tea protecting my mama's mahogany drum table for the better part of four decades, abruptly changed formats.

Oh vile corporate America, which takest away my dream! And, paradoxically, giveth me a strange urge to write in some kind of faux Biblespeak.

Enough of that, ye-all.

I just want to up and cry!

No matter where my writing jobs led, I always felt that the Holy Grail would be to write the program synopses for *TV Guide*. It wasn't my fallback, it was my dream job and, now, verily, it will never be.

As a small and admittedly weird child, I whiled away numerous hours scribbling possible program descriptions for imaginary episodes of my favorite TV series. And I never stopped.

For *Gunsmoke*: "A mysterious stranger threatens to disrupt the annual Calf Rope Festival in Dodge City." For *Friends*: "Hilarity ensues when Ross and Joey switch identities for a day." For *Lost*: "The freakish tropical polar bear devours all the island inhabitants except a whiny blonde who is deemed too scrawny to bother with."

I pictured being paid a big pile of money to watch hundreds of hours of TV before reducing a complicated plot line to a few powerful nouns and verbs.

I practiced by comparing my work with the ones in the real *TV Guide* and usually I liked mine better. Some people are blessed with the ability to cure disease or invent life-saving technology for people in third-world countries. I am blessed to be able to succinctly convey the perfect distillation of pathos and humor in any given episode of *The Suite Life of Zack and Cody*.

Sadly, as we all now know, my gift will never be used because of the format change which makes *TV Guide* just another idiot periodical that I positively can't put down.

In making the change, the publishers announced that TV listings would shrink 75 percent, leaving more room for stories about the stars, TV trends, reviews, and other stuff we could get in a gazillion other places. I'm sorry; did that sound bitter?

And what's with the new inferior *TV Guide*'s obsession with *American Idol*?

It will probably shock y'all to read this but I have never watched a single episode of *American Idol*. Nope. Not one. Never, ever.

Is there help for people like me? People who don't know but only hear snippets about some nasty Brit named Simon or rumors of loopy behavior by Paula Abdul? And what, pray tell, is a Ryan Seacrest?

The truth is, I need *TV Guide* just to be able to function in polite society and pretend to be an "idolator." Everyone I know, and I mean everyone, even the old man who smokes through a hole in his throat at the produce stand, is obsessed with *AI*.

I'm like, "Are these peppers really three for a dollar?" and he's like (growly as always) "Kelly Pickler got robbed last night," and I'm like, "Who?" and he's like, "You can't shop here anymore." At least I think that's what he was saying.

Perhaps I can't relate to *Idol* because I'm such a crappy singer myself. Although, and I don't like to brag, absolutely no one can touch my steamed-up shower version of Billie Holiday's "Good Morning Heartache." It's idolicious!

As self-appointed pop-culture high priestess, I do need *TV Guide* to speak intelligently when Mandisa is voted off the island or whatever the idolators do, but that doesn't mean I like the new format.

The revamped *TV Guide* looks so, well, ordinary. Jerry Seinfeld once observed that no one ever handed anyone a *TV Guide*. The compact little magazine was always thrown. Was there any other magazine you can think of that could sail across a den so magnificently? I thought not.

TV Guide was, for five decades, incredibly and undeniably aerodynamic. Now we are forced to throw *Reader's Digest* across the room but it's just not the same. I've tried it. And, yes, I do realize how pathetic that sounds.

So who really killed *TV Guide*? As nutty as it sounds, the magazine did itself in when it provided on-screen program guides for cable companies.

Predictably, quality has suffered. For two weeks in a row recently, I was subjected to this electronic program guide description of my beloved *Days of our Lives*: "Relationships grow and die in the fictional town of Salem."

That's it? Are you kidding me? What about something a little more worthy of the very name *TV Guide*? Let's see if I've still got "the gift." Ah, yes! How about "A frantic Samantha fears her fiancé, Lucas, will call off their wedding when he realizes she was once a man"?

Synopsis: As coaster, as airplane, as guide to freakin' life, I will always miss the real *TV Guide*.

It's selfish to whine about losing my dream job when so

many of the big names in television are suffering just as much.

Poor Dan Rather quit CBS in a huff after the network dissed him by essentially giving the award-winning anchor and watery-eyed veteran of innumerable national calamities an office the size of a Cheez-It with instructions not to use the phone for personal calls.

After all those years, Rather's famously folksy turns of phrase were no longer welcome at the Big Eye. Which made me madder than a mule chewing on a wasp nest, by the way.

TV can be a cruel medium. Look at the rise and fall of Star Jones, one-time humble McDonald's fry girl turned brilliant court reporter turned voracious man-eating, weight-losing, fur-wearing Bridezilla.

Barbara Walters, 105, said that she was just sick about Star's sudden exit from *The View* because she and co-hosts Elizabeth Hasselbeck and Joy Behar had been planning all along to simply feed the suddenly diminutive Star to *View* add-on Rosie O'Donnell during sweeps month.

"The timing sucked on this one," said Babs.

When watching *The View*, which I periodically do if dragged into a room and my eyelids are glued open a la *A Clockwork Orange*, I want to feel like I'm with my posse, my gal-pals, sipping Cointreau margaritas and bitching about our menfolk.

I'm ashamed to say it but I liked Star better fat. She bought her shoes at Payless, for heaven's sake. How much more real and girlfriendy can you get?

But Star got skinny and greedy and committed the ultimate

tacky foul by asking sponsors to pay for her wedding in exchange for a few ham-handed mentions on the show.

Celebrities are terrific at mending battered images, and all Star has to do is go on Oprah's show and apologize for unmitigated tackiness. If that doesn't work, she can always immediately adopt at least one baby from a war-ravaged country or simply borrow one from the perpetually pregnant Heidi Klum.

And speaking of Oprah, I'm officially Over Her.

Over the years, I've sent copies of all of my books to Miss Thang and I've never heard pea-turkey-squat back. Don't get me wrong. I didn't honestly expect to hear anything from O, but I was, as she is so fond of saying, "putting it out there in the universe."

Sadly, my universe apparently ends at O's mailroom and I suspect those books never made it upstairs to the Harpo offices, much less to the rarefied jasmine-scented air of O's personal workspace, which I imagine to look a lot like Willy Wonka's Chocolate Factory with lots of tiny, little Oprah helpers scurrying about and doing her bidding.

I never even got the pre-stamped autographed picture of O advising me to "Live Your Best Life!" or similar drivel.

That said, it was with no small amount of skepticism that I watched Oprah's recent show on *The Secret*. I practiced writing a *TV Guide* synopsis in my head just for old time's sake but it came out sounding bitter: "Oprah reveals the secret to the perfect life based on the rants of author Rhonda Byrne and a panel consisting of a former drug dealer, a recovering slut, and the guy who writes the *Chicken Soup* books."

Oprah's panel of geniuses agreed that you can get anything you want in life by simply thinking, feeling, and acting positive.

Shit. All I'd done was use correct postage. No wonder she never responded to my books.

Watching the panel of "Secret" experts, I realized that my negative energy had ensured that Oprah would never read any of my books. My dismal failure to attract O was my own fault. I had turned Oprah into Noprah.

How, you ask?

Well, that's easy. Hadn't I said to the woman at the post office, "Here goes *nothing*!" and "Great. Another $5.47 down the frikkin drain" when I mailed them to Chicago?

According to *The Secret*, I should've said to the postal clerk: "This book is going to be delivered personally to Oprah Winfrey's hands and she is going to read it and love it and endorse it and soon I will be able to hire a personal assistant and I won't have to stand here and wait in this line full of loser assholes and *watch the hair on my legs get longer*. . . ." Oops, sorry, that whole positive energy thing isn't really my strong suit.

And, because everybody listens to Oprah and has run out, purchased, and is now living by *The Secret*, the postal clerk will smile lovingly at me and say, "You're absolutely right! Oprah is going to love this book and you are going to have a great life and I am too because now that I have *The Secret* I no longer daydream about plunging an oyster knife into my husband's ear while he sleeps."

Well, all righty then.

Bottom line: I'm re-submitting my books to Oprah and happily visualizing them flying off the shelves because, as the former drug dealer or maybe it was the ex-ho said, "like attracts like."

I'm also taking the wisdom of *The Secret* to heart and reminding myself out loud every day that "I. Am. Phenomenal." And because I have put all these positive thoughts into the universe, I have become a human vessel filled with gratitude and forgiveness.

Who is going to be really pissed if this crap doesn't work.

Dang, there I go again with all that negative stuff. My friend and Sunday School teacher, Beth, says that whenever she has a negative thought, she just snaps a rubber band that she wears on her wrist to remind her to shake off the bad thoughts and be more positive. If I'm being honest, Beth's solution, which costs less than a penny a week, seems like a much more economical solution than buying *The Secret* book, accompanying ninety-minute DVD, and signing up for *Secret* seminars at the local Ramada where everybody is just as big a loser as you.

Watching Oprah carry on about *The Secret* during two entire episodes made me want to shake her and remind her that she's from "Miss-sippi." Maybe she's been living in Chicago too long. In the South, we are innately skeptical of this sort of drivel. We're still smarting from buying all those "lightning rods" that still sit on top of some of our houses, not to mention those anointed "prayer cloths" that the TV preacher swore would make our bunions go away.

In the immortal words of George W. Bush, "fool me once, shame on you; fool me twice, shame on you again. Naw, that's not right; fool me twice and, oh, what the hell, we won't get fooled again."

We're over it; we know life isn't that simple (we have the bunions and burned-out home place to prove it). To buy into *The Secret* is admitting that I believe that all I got to do to get dinner on the table is to put out there in the universe that I'd like some meatloaf, snap beans, and fresh corn to materialize onto my family's plates long about 6 P.M. like we're the freakin' Jetsons. Not gonna happen.

To hear *Secret* head cheerleader and author Rhonda Byrne tell it, all we have to do to get anything we want (weight loss, perfect health, fame, fortune, early '90s Dennis Quaid when he looked really hot, etc.) is to "become that which you want on the inside and you shall receive it in the outside world."

My big ass.

Speaking of which, why don't I just *Secret* my way to trading in my lumpy carcass for the the perky posterior of a twenty-year-old aerobics instructor? I'm putting it out there in the universe. Unfortunately, it's gonna be fighting with the heart-felt wish for a pan of homemade peach cobbler that I also just put out there. Yes, hons, that's right: It's a perky ass vs. peach cobbler SmackDown. Then again, why choose? I can have it all, as long as I "ask and believe, I will receive," says Byrne.

Besides, Byrne says overweight people get that way from

"thinking fat thoughts." That's precisely the sort of noodle-brained logic I'd expect from a woman who looks like she weighs ninety pounds soaking wet.

No, Sugar, they get that way from eating macaroni and cheese at the Cracker Barrel five times a week and twice't on Sunday.

Even though *The Secret* smacks of hooey and hokum to most God-fearing Southerners, I'm sure there are a few who are thinking it's worth a try if it helps them get a husband with a trust fund or a boat slip in the best marina.

Even my best redneck friend, Dempsey, says he's using *The Secret* to get a new bass boat. Face it, y'all: When rednecks embrace *The Secret,* that tells me that it has done gone mainstream.

"I just sit around and picture me sitting in that bass boat," says Dempsey, whose wife, Lo-Retta, turned him onto changing the universe with his mind after seeing Oprah on the TV at the Laundromat one fateful afternoon.

Lo-Retta admitted that changing the universe with his mind might be ambitious for someone who has trouble remembering to change his underwear, but she's proud of all the positive magnetism her husband is projecting.

"My Dempsey is just eat *up* with positivity," she told me one day.

Because a big part of *The Secret* is being prepared for the inevitable granting of wishes and goals, Dempsey has laid in a stock of PBRs and Slim Jim beef jerky sticks to take out on the boat when it arrives.

"You have to be ready for the fulfillment of your magnet-ism," Dempsey said. "The laws of attraction are all that governs our entire universe."

"What does that really mean?" I asked.

"Shit if I know," said Dempsey.

Somewhere, Rhonda Byrne is laughing her bony ass off.

26

French Women Suck at Competitive Eating

U nlike Al Gore, we women spend an inordinate amount of time worried about our weight. Like many women, I'm a yo-yo dieter, putting it on and taking it right back off, then putting it on again and taking about half of it right back off. I know. The math isn't good, is it?

I have to tell you that the fastest dieting success I've ever had was with the fabulous and famous French Women's Diet, where you eat tiny portions of things you love along with lots of red wine.

I dropped twelve pounds in three months using the French

Women's Diet but the German woman within spent the next twelve months pummeling French woman into strudel and all the weight is back.

Oh, well. I can't say it wasn't fun. My German/Swiss heritage leaves me most of the time not knowing whether to say "yes" to another round of brats, or simply yodel.

I'd been inspired by the book *French Women Don't Get Fat*, which stresses tiny portions of wonderful things. Inside my body, it was as if a real French woman had taken up residence. I imagined her petulant and puny, even trying desperately to get me to take up smoking again. When I was observing the French Women's Diet, I ate like Nicole Richie sans the Vicodin buffet.

But German woman would have none of it. As the months passed and the pounds slowly and steadily piled back on, I imagined a sort of internal SmackDown between the French woman with her long eyelashes and perpetually bored expression and the German woman, ruddy-cheeked and precious in a starched apron, simply urging me to have that second pound of hot potato salad.

Occasionally, my Swiss heritage would remind me that it was time for yet another cup of cocoa. Yo-dee-lay-ee-o!

"Acck! You're not going to drink that without marshmallows, are you?" the German woman within would remind me while, I imagined, wiping her sturdy flour-dusted hands on her apron.

"You vill die vat and unattractive," hissed the French woman, while licking a microscopic piece of cheese.

I can pinpoint the precise moment at which I finally kicked

the French woman to the curb. It was over lunch with my friend, Nan. I was having my usual: a single leaf of romaine and a very large unsweetened tea. Nan was having a meatball sandwich and a side of fries.

I could tell she had something on her mind. Finally, she looked me dead in the eye and said, "You've lost too much weight; your face is looking too old."

Now you might say to yourself, what kind of friend is that? And I'd say, the very best and dearest kind there is.

You don't need no stinkin' intervention with a friend like Nan. I immediately summoned the waitress and ordered a huge plate of pasta with sausage and peppers. From somewhere deep inside of me, I heard a muffled squeal of horror from the French woman. It wasn't like I'd developed twin personalities, exactly, but I'd kind of gotten to like "Gigi," as I called her. What? Like you've never had an imaginary friend living inside of you?

From that day forward, it was full-scale war. Eventually, the American woman came in to lend German woman a hand from time to time in the form of fried mushrooms with ranch dressing dip.

And the rest, as they say, is history.

Once I realized that it was possible to lose weight on the French Women's Diet anytime I wanted, I toyed with the notion of competitive eating.

It's not as bizarre as it sounds. The winners of those contests are almost never fat. In fact, most of them are tiny, like world record holder and Polly Pocket–sized Sonya "The Black

Widow" Thomas, who once devoured 432 oysters in ten minutes.

What a woman! When I read about Sonya, let's just say that I felt a lot less guilty about sampling all five desserts on the Golden Corral buffet that one time.

OK, every time.

Sonya, who weighs just 100 pounds, trains for competitions and makes tons of money when she wins. She goes to all-you-can-eat buffets to stretch her stomach.

Competitive eating really is a sport or ESPN wouldn't cover it, right? This brings an almost virtuous spin to the All You Can Eat concept. If you hog all the hushpuppies at Captain Gnarly's Big Barge of Chum Buffet & Fish Camp, you can always shrug, point to your bulging midsection, and say, "In training, you know."

In an interview, Sonya admitted that "Probably sixty percent of the people out there think competitive eating is really stupid." Not to quibble, hon, but I suspect it's closer to ninety-five percent. Still, I hate to argue with a woman who can eat eleven pounds of cheesecake in nine minutes. She so rocks!

Imagine Sonya joining my pals for our monthly Girls Night Out, where we all divide a key lime tart no bigger than a jar lid into six pieces while squealing about how full we are.

"You disgust me," she would say while demolishing eight pounds of margarine.

Competitive eaters are never from France, for obvious reasons, but there are many from Asia and the United States. One of the most famous is Takeru "The Tsunami" Kobayashi, who earned $150,000 in contest winnings. To the people who say it's not a legit sport, Takeru is laughing all the way to the bank. Puking and laughing, that is.

Takeru ate fifty hot dogs in twelve minutes and seventeen pounds of cow brains in fifteen minutes. He trains by eating only cabbage and water before competitions and, one hopes, staying far, far away from family and friends.

As a Southerner, though, my allegiance must remain with Carson "Collard Greens" Hughes of Tennessee, who wolfed 2.5 pounds of cooked collards in seventeen seconds. His aunt said he did it at home all the time, "never leaving nothing for the young'uns to fight over."

There's even a mayonnaise-eating contest coming up, according to the competitive eating events calendar, which I subscribe to, just in case.

If I can beat the world record of eating four quarts in eight minutes, I could earn cash and a nifty nickname like "Jiffy Lube."

Maybe we should all think about eating as much as we can stuff into ourselves right now because, according to scientists, millions of honeybees are dying off and if it keeps going like this, we'll basically run out of food by the year 2012.

Which means, you guessed it, we'll be stuck eating Lunchables.

Last night, I lost sleep fretting about the dwindling bee population. They're just dropping dead and nobody knows why, not even Al Gore, who has gotten so distressed about it, he's gained another forty-five pounds just in worry weight.

If he doesn't watch out, he's going to replace button-nosed has-been Valerie Bertinelli as Jenny Craig's new spokesmodel. Of course, Al would be a huge downer because he'd take his little melting polar ice caps charts and graphs everywhere with him. He is *so* party buzz kill.

Then again, without the bees, there won't be any food of any kind so we'll all pretty much look like Mischa Barton who, as my Uncle Peanut likes to point out, "hasn't got enough fat on her ass to fry her own ears."

Just since I started writing this, another 40,000 bees have died. Are you worried now? You bloody well should be because scientists say that by pollinating our fruits and vegetables, bees are responsible for every third bite of food we eat. More if you're a simple-minded bear who wears an entirely too small red shirt and no pants.

The problem, dubbed "colony collapse disorder," seems to be that bees go out in search of nectar and pollen just like they always have but they never come back. It's as if a giant bee Rapture has taken place, except I'm fairly certain bees aren't even particularly religious.

Years ago, I was friends with a woman whose husband left for a carton of milk and never came back. Turns out he had a little extracurricular pollinating of his own to take care of. No loss there.

But bees? They're really important, y'all, and not just because in another five to ten years, you might actually have to buy another one of those bear-shaped plastic bottles of honey. (Why don't they put honey in little bottles the size of nail polish? At least that way you wouldn't be looking at that weird white crud that forms on the top of the bottle after about year four.)

So what the hell is killing the bees? Some scientists have deduced that the problem is that they're "stressed out," which sounds ridiculous to me because it's not as if they've ever had an adjustable rate mortgage.

Yes, I love bees now, because I realize how hard they've been working for us all these years. Except for the carpenter bees. They're still assholes.

Maybe all this means that the bees are going to put us all on an involuntary weight-loss program called starvation. And while I'm not looking forward to it, and it's certainly going to ruin my budding competitive eating career, it may be the only way to get those Ambien druggies to shape up.

A study found that some people who take the sleeping pill gain more than 100 pounds because they're eating in their sleep.

From now on, when I gain a few pounds, I'll just hang my head and say, "Hey, it was either get a good night's sleep or gain a little weight. I chose sleep. Don't judge me!"

Perhaps the weirdest finding was that these folks aren't simply foraging around for a banana or a cookie while dead asleep; no, no! They're actually preparing full meals!

I can't even cook that great when I'm awake and these fools are, like, torching crème brûlée and braising meat while they're asleep. WTF?

I read an interview with a woman who had gained more

than 100 pounds by cooking while asleep. Every morning, girlfriend was mystified by the dirty dishes and empty refrigerator.

In the South, we usually just figure that the waterbugs got especially industrious overnight. Those suckers are *big*. It's not a huge stretch for me to assume that, one night, they'll just walk upstairs and ask me, in waterbug-speak, "Yo, girl, where's the FryDaddy? Me and the kids is hawn-gry!"

Of course Ambien doesn't just make you cook and eat while asleep. There are documented findings that some people who take Ambien actually have sex and don't remember it. They're called *married people*.

At this rate, anything and everything that goes wrong is being blamed on Ambien, although I'm going to miss my standard: "It's because we have a Republican Congress."

Researchers have even found that, besides cooking and eating and screwing, Ambien users occasionally drive in their sleep.

I'm so using that one the next time I get stopped for speeding. I'm going to tell the policeman that it wasn't my fault because I'm technically sound asleep and no one can be expected to observe the rules of the road while simultaneously dreaming that they have just had a litter of kittens with Patrick Dempsey.

Yeah. That should work.

27

No, Really; Why Can't We Spay Tori Spelling?

❧

The woman on the other end of the phone wanted to know if I was a registered voter and, if so, would I mind answering a few questions.

"It will only take a few moments of your time," she chirped. "And it's for a very important cause."

"Really?" I asked. "Is somebody finally going to invent a pair of gauchos that won't make it look like I'm pregnant in my butt?"

"Uh, no." Nervous laughter.

"Spaying and neutering your pets?"

"No."

"Spaying and neutering Tori Spelling?"

"Huh?"

"Sorry, just having a little fun. Please continue."

"I just want to ask you a few questions that pertain to the upcoming state senate race."

"Wait a minute," I said. "Meemaw's visiting today. Maybe you should talk to her. She hasn't missed voting in a single election since FDR."

"Well," she said, "I guess that would be OK."

"Oops, too late. We can't bother her right now because the *Wheel*'s just come on and she thinks Pat Sajak is sending her messages through the television. Looks like you're stuck with me."

"OK, then. First question: Would you describe yourself as a liberal, moderate, or conservative?"

"Well, I don't really like labels. Let's just say I'm a Virgo."

"But, generally speaking, would you say that you are more a proponent of liberal or conservative causes?"

"Aquarius."

"We can come back to that one," she said, still remarkably perky. "How about this one? Would you be less inclined to vote for (Senator X) if you knew that she had, while working as a lawyer in private practice, once defended a murderer?"

"What kind of boneheaded question is that? She's a criminal defense attorney. Isn't she just doing her part to make sure that every defendant has representation? Isn't the right to a fair trial guaranteed by the Constitution?"

(Smugly) "So you're a liberal."

"I didn't say that. I just said that the question is ignorant."

"Ooooh, a flag-burning liberal!"

"What?!"

"Let's move on. Would you be more or less inclined to vote for (Senator X) if you knew that she had supported stem-cell research?"

"More."

"Ooooh, a flag-burning, baby-killing liberal!"

"What?!"

"One more question. Would you be more or less inclined to vote for (Senator X) if you knew that she had once bitten the head off a live chicken while she was high on LSD?"

"What?"

"LSD. It was a very popular hallucinogen back in the 70s, which, coincidentally, is exactly when (Senator X) was a teenager."

"No, I know what LSD is. . . ."

"Of course you do."

"No, not like that, what I mean is I finally get it!"

"Get what?"

"That this is one of those polls where you say all this made-up inflammatory stuff about one candidate so people will remember it and vote for your guy right? Does anybody really ever fall for that?"

I hung up the phone before she could answer and went to check on Meemaw, who was clucking disgustedly at a political ad for (Senator X).

"What's wrong with her?" I asked.

"Have you been living with Osama under a rock, girl? Everybody knows she gets high and bites the heads off live chickens."

"She does not! That's just a smear campaign. It's what those people do all the time. They make up lies and then they tell them so many times that everybody starts believing them."

I was wasting my time arguing politics with Meemaw because she's old-school. That, and how much do you really want to argue with someone who's convinced, no matter how many times you correct her, that Vanna White used to play Elly May on *The Beverly Hillbillies*?

But it seriously irked me that these "push polls" were actually working on people.

I already knew the country was going to shit when I read that former FEMA Director Michael Brown had opened a consulting business to help clients handle large-scale emergencies.

This, coming off his stellar Brownie-like handling of Katrina called to mind a very old joke: "I didn't used to be able to spell disaster management specialist and now I are one."

Was Brownie was on the pipe? There was simply no other plausible explanation.

Did he seriously think that anyone in his right mind would *pay him money* to teach them how to handle a crisis? I wouldn't trust this guy to pick up my dry-cleaning without screwing it up.

Not long before Brownie was finally and mercifully excommunicated from the White House, I was struck by his creepily out-of-place frat-boy demeanor. Remember how he whined to reporters that he was missing "really good Mexican food" down there in what used to be New Orleans?

He said that just as soon as he got the OK from the big guy, he was going to go home, grab the little woman, and have himself a margarita and some chimichangas.

Speaking as someone who has occasionally been criticized for being as sensitive as a toilet seat, even I had trouble with that one, considering he was stumbling over dead bodies at the time.

And don't forget he's the same guy who fretted endlessly via e-mail with a female staffer about the style of shirt he should wear on camera. Gee, I dunno, Brownie. I liked you in the blue Oxford cloth with the nifty FEMA logo on the breast pocket. The red Polo, while earnestly casual in a Circuit City employee kind of way, just didn't seem right. Perhaps if there could have been a shirt with the words "Dunderheaded Incompetent" stitched on the front. Ahhhh, perfect.

But all should be forgiven because, sadly, we Americans don't harbor a grudge nearly as long as we should. And that propensity to forgive and forget has led to Brownie announcing that he's now an emergency expert extraordinaire.

This is a little like Tyra Banks claiming to have the interviewing skills of Ted Koppel.

In announcing his new gig, Brownie said that he'll counsel officials on how to learn what's going on in a disaster so they won't "appear unaware of how serious a situation is."

But of course. It's all about appearance, right? It's OK if you're clueless, say a real Arabian horse's ass, as long as nobody figures that out.

Brownie says he's already got some clients lined up. You can hardly detect their lobotomy scars.

What's next? Billy Joel teaching driver's education classes? Michael Richards and Don Imus team-teaching on race relations? Tara Reid teaching, well, anything?

Just when I think the far right has bottomed out, though, they come up with something even more bizarre than Brownie becoming a disaster consultant.

The latest target of the mouth-foaming, self-righteous right? The American Girl dolls.

Yes, I can scarcely believe it myself, but it's true. When I first heard that a boycott had been launched against the squeaky-clean American Girl dolls on moral grounds, I assumed that Samantha, Nellie, and Josefina had gotten caught in a three-way, but then I realized that none of them are Carolina Panthers cheerleaders so that couldn't be it.

Had Felicity and Elizabeth turned their 1774 tea room into a meth lab, and were they cooking up something decidedly less nutritious than Felicity's favorite flummery dessert?

How can conservatives hate the American Girl dolls? It just didn't make sense.

But, as I've said before, in a world where the same people who can't be bothered to vote or read newspapers are scared that a cartoon sponge is going to make their kids gay, I suppose anything is possible.

Around the country, fund-raising American Girl doll fashion shows were canceled because of the boycott.

What had these plucky pioneers and caring orphans done to outrage the radical right? Well, as it turns out, it was all because the company that makes the dolls donated $50,000 from the sale of "I Can" bracelets to Girls Inc.

Girls Inc. is a venerable organization that has offered after-school and summer programs to girls, often underprivileged ones, for decades.

But that's good, right?

Wrong, you pointy-headed, free-range-chicken–eating, Prius-driving liberal nut job.

Don't you know nothing about hate-mongering?

You see, a few moms found out by reading the Girls Inc. Web site that, besides offering support and empowerment for girls and young women, Girls Inc. states its supports for girls who might be questioning their sexual identity (whoops, there it is!) and also mentions the organization's support for Roe v. Wade.

Score! Double whammy! It's just a perfectly logical step to deduce that Molly and Kit won't be worried about the Great Depression or World War II, as their homespun biographies suggest. Oh, no, they'll be taking Samantha to the abortion clinic. Then, maybe later, they'll have that three-way.

So the boycott is on and parents like me, who have a daughter with American Girl dolls she loves and a birthday wish list full of A.G. accessories—must now ask themselves some pretty heavy questions. Or not.

I had to admit that I was plenty relieved when the Princess switched her allegiance from the vile Bratz dolls to A.G.s. She still liked the big-eyed hos but the simple homespun goodness of American Girl dolls seemed to be winning.

To this day, the funniest sight is seeing those dolls share shelf space in Soph's room. Wholesome waif Nellie, in demure gray coat with matching hat and mittens, is flanked by two of the skankiest looking Bratz dolls you'll ever see.

At night, I imagine the bad girls having a lot of fun at Nellie's expense. Sort of a pay-per-view American Girl/Bratz Smack-Down. Ratings would be through the roof.

And nightly conversations might go something like this:

Bratz 1: "Hey Prairie Face, let me fix your hair. You could use some extensions or at least some spray glitter, for real."

Nellie: "Oh, no thank you, my rowdy whore-like friend. I'm going to spend the evening teaching deaf children how to sign so I have no necessity for fancy hair adornments."

Bratz 2: "You can't disrespect my friend that way, Laura Ingalls Weirdo."

Nellie: "Felicity!!! Help!!!"

Felicity: "Oh, prithee we all just settle this with a nice cup of tea! Grandfather says that there is no argument that can't be disrupted for a fine pot of chamomile."

Bratz 1: "Never mind that, but I'll take some Red Bull and Hennessy if you got it."

Nellie: "Red Bull? Hennessy? I fear I do not know of these refreshments."

Felicity (whispering): "I believe they call it crunk juice. Grandfather says it will make you behave quite strangely and that we should most certainly give it a wide berth."

Bratz 2: "Who're you calling wide, apronhead?"

Bratz 1: "Don't ya'll ever sneak out of the house? I mean look at you two. Your dresses are all down around your knees; your stockings ain't even torn."

Nellie: "I think we need a mediator here. Prithee, is our friend Barbie in the house?"

Barbie: "Hi everyone! Excuse the limp. I lost a leg during an altercation with Yasmin Bratz the other night. She's one tough cookie!"

Felicity: "Prithee, where was Blaine, or even Ken? Couldn't they protect you?"

Barbie: "No, they were busy that night. They rented that movie *Brokeback Mountain*. Ken said the cinematography was fabulous!"

Bratz 2: "Are y'all just ignerant or what? Those fools are playing you!"

Felicity: "Prithee . . ."

Bratz 1: "Stop sayin' that word, you triflin' heifer."

Nellie: "Oh! Look! It's almost daybreak. Let's not fight anymore. I hate conflict as much as I hate the wrenching poverty brought on by the Great Depression, don't you?"

Bratz 1 & 2: . . .

Felicity and Nellie: "OK, then, tonight. I'll bring the gingersnaps and you two can bring the cider!

Bratz 1: "How about we just bring our pimp? I think he'd like to meet you two."

Felicity and Nellie (nervously): "Fiddlesticks!"

28

Kissin' Up to the Insurance Company

☙

My husband's car was totaled recently by a dumbass drunk driver. The silver lining, besides the fact that hubby didn't get seriously hurt, was that we never knew how many friends we had until this accident happened.

While very few of our actual friends inquired about hubby's health in the days after the accident, I am happy to report that a caring cadre of lawyers and chiropractors stepped in to fill the void and filled our mailbox with mushy letters of concern and compassion.

The bushel basketful of letters sat in our foyer overflowing with offers of help and advice (with absolutely *no* obligation). It was far too heavy to lift so we just kept tossing the new letters on top. When they reached the ceiling, we planned to just rent a backhoe and a Dumpster (y'all know I've missed having one) and start all over again.

Who says the milk of human kindness has curdled? Not so! Personally, I haven't been this popular since I took cupcakes with gummy worms baked inside to my kid's kindergarten class.

Some of the more considerate lawyers included little refrigerator magnets as gifts so we would think of them every time we opened the fridge door. ("Hmmm, honey, we're almost out of Go-Gurt, but boy, oh, boy, something is really making me feel *litigious* today!")

The lawyer letters were fun to read. One boasted of a huge staff ready to serve us with toll-free phone numbers, private cell numbers, and rental cars delivered at the speed of sound. All we had to do is ask. Plus *hablamos español*, whatever the hell that means.

A no-frills lawyer claimed to have no staff at all and was therefore always ready to work on our case and our case only. This dedication would take place from the front seat of his 1993 Ford Focus and could I please bring my own laptop. Or we could "meet at Kinko's conference room where sometimes there's free coffee." Not a big confidence-instiller, dude.

The chiropractic letters were, unfortunately, not as imaginative. Since they all said the same thing, I think the docs should have offered something more: perhaps the "So You've

Been Hit by an Asshole Free Pizza" coupon or a bottle opener shaped like a skeleton where the skull snaps off the bottle cap, red eyes light up, and it screams "Drunk drivers *suck!*" Y'all would so have our business.

Most chiropractors included a questionnaire asking if hubby had any "feelings of anxiety" after the wreck. Of course not. There's nothing about losing your finally-paid-for car, and wondering how you're going to buy another one for the roughly $53.18 the insurance company is willing to kick in, that would promote feelings of anxiety now is there?

Kidding! We were sure the insurance company would take care of us and do the right and moral thing and that we would be fairly and speedily compensated for the vehicle loss as well as any unexplained pain radiating from the shoulders to the fingertips accompanied by tingling of all extremities heretofore or unmentioned in perpetuity so help us God.

So we met with our insurance guy and that's when we found out that the drunk asshole was insured by the same company as us.

"But isn't that like some kind of conflict of interest?" I asked the insurance adjuster assigned to our claim.

"Oh, now, someone has been talking to a lawyer, hasn't someone? Let's do this without lawyers, OK? I am prepared to offer you this number (scribbles number on paper and shoves it across the desk to us just like they do in the movies).

We chuckled.

"I believe you left off some digits, dude," I said. "You expect him to get to work via pogo stick?"

"Pogo stick! Ha! That's funny. I thought you might say that. So (with a flourish of pen and paper), how about *this*?"

We went through this a few more times and we finally realized that there was no way we'd ever get enough money to replace the car that had been demolished.

It didn't seem remotely fair, so we decided to get a lawyer to at least scare the monkeyshit out of the insurance company a little bit. In the end, we got double the amount on the first little piece of paper (yes, enough for *two* pogo sticks!) but the whole thing left a bad taste.

Plus, we had to go car-shopping. This is always an agonizing experience because I like cute and blue and hubby likes big and engine that works. Bor-ing. We went to a few car dealerships before we finally found the right deal (and a cute-as-pie salesman who never *once* asked, "Now what's it gonna take to get you in a car *today*?")

Along the way, though, we dealt with a few car salesmen that seemed to have taken the touchy-feely thing too far.

One salesman, who had a very thick French-sounding accent, shook hubby's hand, then leaned in to kiss me on the cheek.

"Whoa, dude," I said. "That may be how they do it in Europe, but you're in Amurica now, boy."

He grinned and then kissed my hand, which was also creepsome.

Have you noticed how people are kissing more and shaking hands less? No less than *The New York Times* says that the kiss is replacing the handshake in some business circles.

I hate this trend because everybody gets the kiss thing wrong. They go for the wrong cheek and collide at the lips (horrors!) or one person goes for the double-cheek Euro kiss while the weary recipient just stands there waiting for it to please stop.

According to *The Times*, the Swiss routinely kiss a minimum of three times on each cheek, leaving very little time to actually make chocolate or obnoxious clocks, it seems to me.

The phenomenon is being discussed and debated with etiquette experts telling us how to properly kiss and be kissed in a business setting. And while I have been accused of kissing the boss' ass in the workplace, I can assure you it was purely metaphorical and, by the way, sir, may I say that your new haircut makes you look at least ten years younger?

Car salesmen kissing my hand? Wrong location, dude.

But you can't blame him for trying.

Even the insurance adjuster seemed flustered by whether he should shake hands or offer me a quick peck on the cheek when it came time to pick up the check.

A handshake, etiquette experts say, is just considered too stodgy these days. Oh yeah? Why stop at just a kiss? Why not just *get a room*?

I live in the South, y'all, where men have the whole handshake, polite nod, and manly hug with backslap combo thing down. They don't need to learn anything new because they've just gotten comfy with the high-five-turned-into-bear-hug-with-arms-between-stomachs maneuver.

I don't want to belabor the point, but it's scary when real

etiquette experts say that kisses can be useful if you work in sales.

Note to Best Buy salesman: Kissing isn't going to make me buy that extended warranty so back the hell off.

Today it's kissing, tomorrow it's lap dances with the controller. Don't say I didn't warn you.

Because hubby had been hit by two dumbass drunk drivers in the past, he was determined to get a really big car and, although I could hear Sheryl Crowe silently sobbing in the background, I was totally down with it.

Sadly, because it was so big, and pricey, we had a car payment again, or to be precise, seventy-two of 'em.

Meanwhile, drunk asshole was probably on the road again. He had been too drunk to actually get injured, though his car had also been demolished. As he crawled out of the wreckage, hubby said his first words were vintage redneck: "Dude, help me get these beer bottles outta here before the cops come."

"Yeah," said hubby, while he counted his extremities. "I'll get right on that."

I'm hopeful for fewer wrecks in the future though. Toyota is rolling out a new car that detects if you've had too much to drink. This "smart car" works by analyzing the amount of booze in your palm sweat so if your drunk ass tries to drive, the car will simply refuse to start. And while Mel Gibson and half the cast of *Lost* are saying, "About damn time," there might be some kinks.

Like, how does it work if you're wearing gloves? No problem, engineers say. The system also kicks in if it detects abnormal steering. There's even a camera that can determine if your eyes are glazed over, as if intoxicated or as if watching any episode of *According to Jim*.

If the smart car decides you're too drunk to drive, it will slowly come to a stop, refuse to start again, and (I'd like to see this little feature added) systematically call everyone you know on your cell phone and inform them what a big wasted loser you are, including your mama and your boss.

Cars are getting way smarter than people; that's not news. But the car becoming the authority figure is taking it to the next level. I'm counting on the Japanese automakers to develop a backseat outfitted with sensors that can tell whether or not your kid is lying when he says he's finished his homework.

Let's say Little Bubba wants to play soccer, so you're on the way to the field to meet his buddies when you casually ask him, "Billy Bob, are you sure you finished all your homework?"

If he says, "Yes," millions of tiny sweat sensors inside the seat will activate and the car will automatically steer itself to the nearest public library for an impromptu study session.

Of course, the car could be programmed to save us from things besides drunk driving and lying young'uns.

Say you're craving a foot-long hot dog and some tater tots from your favorite fast-food joint. You slow down on approach, flip the turn signal and, whoa, what's this? The car inexplicably refuses to turn and delivers you, instead, to (horrors!) the nearest

YMCA, seat sensors having detected that your ass appears to be roughly the size of Poland.

I'm depending on car manufacturers to save us from ourselves, y'all. And I don't mind kissing up to them, a little bit anyway.

29

Now That's Just Rude, Y'all

It's time now to update the latest examples of what I like to call Customer Dis-Service. What's that you say? Define Customer Dis-Service; give three examples? Fine, no problem.

Example No. 1

I recently ordered an item from one of those "as seen on TV" places. I won't tell you the name because I don't want to be sued or have a shadowy figure in a hot pink velour sweat suit hold me down and staple my skull with a million tiny little decorative rhinestones and beads "guaranteed to add excitement to any outfit!"

I realized that ordering this '80s gizmo was pure nostalgia. Perhaps I longed for simpler times, when Olivia Newton-John just wanted to know if I'd ever been mellow, had I ever trrrrriiiiieeed. . . . I was seized with an irrational desire to, uh, dazzle up, "an array of sweaters, hats, dresses, slacks, even school book covers!" with these little multicolored beads, brads, and jewels.

This would be fun for the whole family! I knew it would because the nice lady on TV said so. And how could you not trust a woman with her name stud-set in artificial gemstones across her bosom? I imagined what I could put across my own bosom. Perhaps, "Yeah, they're real" on my 34As. I love irony in fake topaz, don't y'all?

So I called the toll-free number for Customer Dis-Service to order the very reasonably priced ($19.95) dazzling jewelry clothing enhancer.

Things were going OK, except for the fact that one of us was a recording, but at least she sounded pleasant, like the kind of woman who would happily and mindlessly spend an afternoon affixing tiny bits of fake shinies to her jeans pockets, her kids' jackets, her cat's ears, all while watching Michael Ontkean strangle his wife for the bazillionth time on the Oxygen channel.

After a couple of minutes, though, the pleasant-voiced woman started getting whiny and demanding.

She would place my order, perhaps even during my lifetime, but first she wanted to share some information about "fabulous offers that are just too good to pass up!"

The minutes ticked by, with me pressing "2" for "No" to offer after offer. Didn't I want the fifteen extra sets of beads and brads, the "free" Target card and gas card, the dining discounts card, or the super-expensive overnight shipping because what sane human could wait for the lumbering wagon-train approach of standard shipping to get started?

"No!" I finally screamed. "Just place the order you bejeweled bee-atch!"

Pause.

"I'm sorry," said the recorded voice. "I didn't quite understand that last answer. Could you repeat it?"

Oh, most assuredly. She wasn't real, after all. I laid her out and each time she came back for more, always calm: "I didn't quite understand that last answer. Could you repeat it?"

After a while it wasn't fun anymore. I pressed a few more "2"s to decline a "spectacular one-time-only" time-share offer. Of course they don't call it "time-share" anymore. That word is about as popular as the phrase "convicted child molester" so they call it "shared ownership" these days.

Minutes ticked by and it was over. The way I'd been treated, I felt like I should roll over and light a cigarette.

No matter. It's done now and all I have to do is watch my mailbox. Which would be much improved with a few sparkly doo-dads by the way.

Example No. 2 (which is really worse)

This may be the best definition of Customer Dis-Service in the history of the airlines.

It seems that a first-class passenger who was taking a nap on a recent British Airways flight from New Delhi to London awoke to find the body of an elderly woman, who had died on the flight while in economy class, strapped into the seat beside him.

Which just goes to show that apparently some people will do anything for an upgrade.

As flight attendants wedged the body into the seat with pillows, because of turbulence, the horrified passenger complained about having to complete the nine-hour flight with a corpse beside him. Granted, the corpse wouldn't be nagging him for the rest of his roasted peanuts, but still.

And here's where the Customer Dis-Service comes in. When he complained, the flight attendants responded, and I quote, "Get over it."

Oh? How exactly?

While some people have said the passenger was insensitive and shallow to complain, you must remember that this was a very long flight. No amount of steaming hot towels, eye shades, courtesy pajamas, and real china and crystal could make up for the fact that there was a body rapidly decomposing in stuffy, recirculated airplane air beside this poor bastard.

Talk about ruining your foie gras. Sitting beside the recently dead can't be soothed by a choice of herbal teas and a nice hot breakfast whilst watching *Wedding Crashers II* in slipperettes.

I don't think the airline handled this very well because they didn't even offer the guy a free ticket. Hell, I got one of those just for agreeing to wait an hour for the next flight to New

York one time. You stick a dead person beside me for nine hours and I'll freakin' *own* your airline.

And, not to be mean about it but, really, since the poor thing was dead, did it really matter whether she flew in first class or economy? How ironic that she probably never got to fly first class in her life and, when she finally did, she was too dead to enjoy it. The fancy noise-blocking headphones, the fabulous choice of individual movies and music channels, the "done been paid for" single-malt Scotch . . . I'm just saying.

Perhaps British Airways should take a cue from Singapore Airlines, which, I swear, has installed "corpse cupboards" on its airliners.

Is it just me or should we all be thinking that flying must be way more dangerous than we thought?

I imagine even the corpse cupboards are different depending on the price of your ticket: a roomy armoire for first-class corpses, a metal school locker for business-class fliers and, for the economy-class corpse, a vacant overhead bin if available or, if not, just a ride up and down the aisles on the bottom tray of the beverage cart for the remainder of the flight.

Which, if you think about it, would give new meaning to the phrase "stiff drink."

Customer Dis-Service is just evidence of a growing culture of crappy behavior that hangs around like a fart in a hot shower.

You can't get rid of it, and the most maddening part of it is when they act like they're doing you a favor.

Which brings me to

Customer Dis-Service No. 3: The Rewards Card Racket.

When the perky clerk at the drugstore asked if I had a "rewards card" I said, "No."

Big mistake. They are trained to shove that rewards card at you as proof how much they value you as a customer. Oh, and if you wouldn't mind signing here, here, here and, yes, right here because we need your phone number, e-mail address, home address, preference in fat-free salad dressings and any damn thing else we can think of.

"Would you like to fill out a rewards card application?" she asked.

"No thanks," I said. "I'm in a bit of a hurry."

"You know," she said (oh, here it comes, the beginnings of a sales-pout), "If you had used a reward card today you could have saved ten percent."

"It was a 3 Musketeers bar and a *National Enquirer,* hon. What would I have saved? Like, four cents?"

"Don't you want to save on future purchases?" (I swear this chick was relentless.)

"Yes," I said, "but I know how this works. Aren't you going to clutter my mailbox and my e-mail with a bunch of useless offers and junk I don't want and sell my personal information to every idiot on the street?"

"Oh, no, ma'am. Just a very few select idiots will get your personal information."

Right.

Look, I'm sick of these "rewards." I don't want the stupid free taco "reward" if I remember to get the card stamped for the first twenty visits. I don't want to work that damn hard for a free taco or seven cents off mouthwash or whatever. Quit giving me stuff to keep me coming back and pretending you're doing me a favor.

If you want to thank me for my business, don't give me one more punchable card, magnetized strip card, or laminated key chain fob that has everything but my damn DNA encoded in it.

Admittedly, my reaction has gotten a bit, uh, animated.

The clerk at the big-box electronics store only gets so far as "Would you . . ." before I scream, "No!"

Sometimes they just flat-out lie to you. At a music store they promised that if I joined their "rewards" program they wouldn't bug me, just send the occasional mailing of sales for "preferred customers." They didn't mention the weekly automated calls to pitch new products, which began almost as soon as I foolishly signed up.

Besides, one would hope that *all* customers are preferred, right?

At my favorite clothing store, they always ask to see my preferred customer card when I check out.

"Does this give me a discount?" I ask.

"Well, no."

"Then, what good is it?"

"It tracks how many times you come in the store."

"So why is this useful to me?"

"Well, sometimes we mail out early notices that we're having a sale."

"Is there a discount?"

"Well, no. But you get to know about the sale before the other customers."

"You mean the un-preferred customers?"

"Well, all of our customers are preferred. We don't want to say that any of them are 'un-preferred.' "

"I prefer not to have to look for a card that doesn't do anything for me but does a lot for you."

"You're weird."

"But I'm the customer! The customer is always right!"

"Who told you that?"

I dunno. Methusaleh?

My theory is that the Customer Dis-Service folks have left us so frustrated that we're all getting more and more hateful.

The other night I went to the movies with duh-hubby and the Princess. It was a decent movie about eight dogs left behind during an Antarctic expedition gone bad. The dogs had a sucky time of it waiting for their human to come back with his gorgeous on-again/off-again girlfriend and rescue them.

Smack in the middle of the movie, a man and woman walked into the theater and loudly asked the woman at the end of our row "How long's this been going?"

She whispered a quick answer and then, to our astonishment, they stood there and weighed their options out loud. Should they sneak into this movie or perhaps another one? Oh, to be a moron and have so many choices.

While the dogs survived on screen by eating frozen whale innards and snagging birds out of the air like Frisbees, Mr. and Mrs. Bonehead chatted and even took time to sit down and call home to check on the kids, who, I'm guessing, weren't nearly as smart as those poor blue-eyed Huskies.

All I'm saying is that we live in an unfair world where perfectly nice dogs have to survive on iced-over gull entrails and rude, noisy moviegoers get to gorge on suitcases of popcorn whenever they like. Opposable thumbs are *so* overrated.

Finally, mercifully, they stood up, dropped their popcorn suitcases loudly on the floor ("I ain't cleaning up, much as they charge for these here movies"), wiped their hands on their sweat pants and announced, "Let's go check out *The Ring Two* 'cause ain't nothing happening here except a buncha snow and shit."

Oh, sadness. Leaving so soon? Don't forget to get your rewards card stamped. For every ten moviegoers you annoy, you get a free trip on British Airways in the Rotting Corpse section. And, if you act before midnight tomorrow, we'll toss in a free bejeweling gizmo to give those sweats some zing!

30

Epilogue

A Queen at Last. . . .

∂

There comes a time in every mature Southern woman's life when she finds herself sitting on a screened porch, a dishpan full of butterbeans waiting to be shelled in her lap, and a gardenia-scented breeze stirring just enough to make her souvenir-of-the-Outer-Banks lighthouse wind chimes go all tinkly-tankly, and she thinks to herself: "It just can't get any better'n this."

Simple pleasures are a Southern woman's divine right. And they can be as simple as pulling a pan of cathead biscuits out of the oven to be served, directly, with turnip greens and chow-chow you made with the bell peppers you picked your own self.

I was that simple soul sitting on the screened porch one day, but then the phone rang and everything changed. And that's when it hit me that sometimes not-so-simple pleasures are equally delicious: I'm going to be a queen, y'all.

Being a queen is the other divine right of every Southern woman and it's a sin and a shame how few of us actually get to do it.

I'm going to be a QUEEN! And not just any queen but the North Carolina Pecan Harvest Festival Queen!

When the festival organizers called to see if I would be their queen, I had one only one question:

"I won't have to wear a bathing suit, will I?"

"Oh, Lord no!" said Bill, the chipper festival coordinator.

"Well you don't have to sound so dang happy about that," I pouted. I'd been a queen for less than twenty-five seconds and was already a diva, bless my heart.

Bill chuckled. "You can wear one if you want to, but it will be in November so you might get chilly riding on that float."

A float?!

I'd only ridden on a float one other time in my life and that was just a couple of years ago in a tiny town in east Texas that was having a book festival. From the back of a decorated flatbed truck, we got to toss beads and Starbursts to an underwhelmed January crowd of about forty.

There was a handmade sign on the side of our "float" that

said "Assorted Authors" (I know; who wouldn't want to brave thirty-degree wind chill for "assorted authors"? I felt like we should be wearing those masks of famous literary figures, like Shakespeare or Nathaniel "Hot 'n' Horny" Hawthorne). A few of the sparsely scattered spectators looked genuinely fearful that we might start conjugating verbs or diagramming sentences or something, but their passion for free beads and candy won out.

But that was just a flatbed truck and I didn't even have a tiara so, clearly, it wasn't really a queenly moment.

But this! This was different.

"You'll be crowned at the luncheon on Friday," said Bill, reading from some notes he'd made for me before the fateful call.

"Can I keep the tiara?"

"Uh, it says here, 'If she asks, tell her she cannot keep the tiara.' "

Whoa. My reputation precedes me.

A little while later, while I was still basking in my future queendom, parade organizer Suzanne called to tell me about my ribbon-cutting duties and how I'd get to reign over the pecan cook-off.

I loved the way Suzanne said "pee-can" instead of the haughtier-than-thou "pe-cahn" which, along with the vile "anyways," is further evidence that Yankees are ruining our Southernspeak one syllable at a time.

Suzanne then told me that I'd be surrounded by eight teenage girls dressed in antebellum gowns with hoop skirts.

"They will comprise your official Queen's Court," she bubbled.

Somebody pinch me; I must be dreamin'.

The use of words like "reign" and "court" were most appealing and I figured that since the pecan belles basically exist to do my bidding, I would instruct them to detail my Taurus while I was in town.

I'm not sure why I was selected to be the North Carolina Pecan Harvest Festival Queen, unless it's because I make a fairly fabulous pecan pie owing to a perfect mix of light and dark Karo syrup and a crust flakier than Drew Barrymore on *Letterman*, don'tchaknow.

I plan to research proper queenly behavior because I could practically hear Bill wince over the phone when I told him in a subsequent call that I'd done a little research and I was pretty sure that we could "kick Georgia's ass" in production next year.

Hey, I've done my homework. I'm no lightweight queen (especially true after I sample ten kinds of homemade pecan tassies, which I can practically taste right now as I write this). Sure, we've produced five million pounds of pecans in a year before, but I think we can do better.

In fact, I'm issuing a royal decree. Yes, unlike poor Kate Middleton, who invested five years of her life trying to be Mrs. Prince William, I'm really going to be royalty.

I realize that it may seem a tad hypocritical of me to embrace my impending queenhood so enthusiastically when I've been known to make fun of pageant queens, but this is different y'all. I was not asked to be North Carolina Pecan Harvest Festival Queen (gawd, no matter how many times I write that, it still gives me goosebumps) because of big boobs (heaven knows) or babbling in the interview segment of some contest about how I want to help adults learn to read 'cause, let's face it, y'all, they really shoulda learned that shit back when they were in school, am I right?

This isn't a beauty contest; it's about wisdom and maturity and, possibly, the ability to speak out when Little Miss Tiny Lower Possum Creek and Surrounding Tributaries won't move her ass out of the way in time for me and my float to get on local TV.

This, I vow and declare, my hons: Although I will be queen for two full days, I won't let it go to my head.

I will still sit and ponder the simple, perfect moments in life on my screened porch and I will nevah, evah forget all the little people who made my reign possible.

Oh, and I'm keeping the tiara, bitches.

Acknowledgments

As always, I am deeply grateful to my fabulous agent, Jenny Bent, of Trident Media, and my incredibly talented editor, Jennifer Enderlin, of St. Martin's Press. Without you two, there would be no new kitchen and I'd be back to writing obits and weddings for a living. Thank-you just doesn't begin to cover it.

Thanks to my precious husband, Scott Whisnant, whom I'm trying hard not to hate on account of he lost twenty-five pounds this year and I found 'em.

I'm grateful every hour of every day for my sweet daughter Sophie. Darling, you are the very reason I get up in the morning. Well, that and the fact that I really have to pee.

Thanks to Lisa Noecker, who understands what it's like to be raised at the edge of a cornfield and want more. For all the "idees" you have given me over the years, I should pay you, but, well, I'm still hoping to add a guest bathroom.

Thanks also to David and Tricia Reid of Vicksburg, Mississippi, whose bravery and humor inspire me more than they could possibly know; and to Miss Sarah Saucier, the smartest seventeen-year-old in Louisiana, who already knows to carry a fried chicken purse into the movies. God help me if she ever starts writing books.

Love to family and friends and to everyone who has taken the time to e-mail me with words of support and ideas for books yet to be written. I am honestly humbled by your kindness and generosity.

—CELIA RIVENBARK
Wilmington, North Carolina